The Science of Living
IN CLASS WITH EMMET FOX

*The original class notes of Dr. Emmet Fox, pastor of
The Church of the Healing Christ, 1931-1951. These were
his personal copies with notations in his handwriting.*

The
Science *of*
Living

In Class with Emmet Fox

Foreword and Supplemental Material by
Revs. JoAnn and Cecil Corsiatto

thegoldenkeys
Farmingdale, New York

Also available

Emmet Fox: His Life Story
by JoAnn Pecoraro Corsiatto, D.Sc.F.
with Cecil Corsiatto

First Edition
First printing, March 2005
Second printing, April 2005
Third printing, May 2005
Fourth printing, June 2005
Fifth printing, July 2005

Printed in the United States of America

Book Production
SPS Publications, Eustis, FL (www.spsbooks.com)
Cover design by Jessica Mitchem

For information on the life and writings of
Dr. Emmet Fox—

Revs. JoAnn & Cecil Corsiatto
Post Office Box 21
Farmingdale, New York 11735

www.emmetfox.net

Dedication

To the students of Emmet Fox—
past, present, and future—for whom
these pages were written.

Contents

Part One

Part Two

The Science of Living

Memories of Emmet Fox

Foreword

In 1931, after many years of speaking for New Thought societies in England, Emmet Fox came to America. At the invitation of Dr. Herman Wolhorn he lectured for the Church of the Healing Christ in New York City. Dr. Wolhorn and the members of the church board of directors were so impressed by Emmet Fox's speaking ability and deep understanding of the Divine Science teachings that they immediately asked him to fill the pulpit of the late Dr. John Murray.

Dr. Murray had been pastor of the Church of the Healing Christ since its inception in August of 1907. It was a unique church, the first to occupy a hotel for a meeting place. It began with seven friends of Dr. and Mrs. Murray, organized as the Society for the Study of Divine Metaphysics. The object of this group was to understand and apply the Truth as taught and practiced by Jesus in the overcoming of sin and the healing of disease. In other words, it was an effort to reestablish what might be called Apostolic Christianity.

The universality of Dr. Murray's message was such that he spoke to each according to their individual need. His audiences were at once overwhelming convinced by his deep love and sincerity. The Society quickly outgrew its initial meeting place in a dining room adjacent to the elevated railroad, where every few minutes the talks had to be suspended while the train passed. A room at the Astor Hotel was obtained to hold services. Eventually, the Society was incorporated under New York law as a Divine Science church. The name for the organization—the Church of the Healing Christ—was adopted at the suggestion of Mrs. Murray. This name came to her when she was restored to health through Christian Science after being diagnosed as hopelessly ill by the best physicians available. Like Dr. Fox, the Murrays were devoted to the study of this new means of healing. In fact, Dr. Murray was the first to inaugurate daily healing meetings in New York.

By the time Emmet Fox came to the Church

of the Healing Christ following the death of Dr. Murray, the congregation had dwindled from thousands to about a hundred. Under his leadership, the church began to grow. Because of his dynamic messages, sincerity and quiet dignity, Dr. Fox's congregation at the Church of the Healing Christ outgrew the ballrooms of the Astor and Biltmore, and later Carnegie Hall, until he had the largest continuous congregation in America. On March 14, 1937, Dr. Fox held services at the Hippodrome Theatre. Later, they moved to the Manhattan Opera House, which had to be enlarged to accommodate the overflowing crowds.

Emmet Fox was born in Ireland on July 30, 1886, into a Catholic family. His family had lived in America prior to his birth; however, his mother had become homesick for Ireland and the family returned just prior to his birth. Emmet's father was a surgeon and a member of British Parliament. He died just before Emmet's twenty-first birthday.

At the early age of eighteen, Emmet Fox had a deep inner calling to help others find peace and healing. While visiting in Cork, Ireland, he came upon a book written by R. Dimsdale

Stocker. This book, he said, was his awakening. Stocker was one of the early teachers of New Thought. Later when Emmet Fox met Dr. Stocker in London, he said he felt like he had met William Shakespeare himself. Fox knew that Dr. Stocker opened his mind to a new way of thinking and living. This was the beginning of his wonderful life journey.

Emmet attended Stamford Hill Jesuit College near London. As he became more aware of the Indwelling Christ, Emmet Fox decided he could not continue his education at the Jesuit school. He then went on to study electrical engineering. Emmet spent the next several years as a practicing electrical engineer, while spending his spare time studying New Thought and speaking for the New Thought societies that had formed in England.

By the time of his arrival in New York, he was an accomplished and magnetic speaker with a thorough understanding of New Thought principles. His services drew thousands of people three times weekly plus Sunday services and hundreds more were turned away for lack of seating. It seemed that everyone wanted to hear to him. It was often said, "He was a teacher who pointed the way to life, love and light." Reports of healings and demonstrations flowed into the church office. During his lifetime, Emmet Fox was a channel for healing all over the world, and his writings are still helping people demonstrate. His books have become best sellers, circulating around the world. More than twelve million people have found new meaning in their lives through the work of this gentle yet profound teacher. After twenty years at the Church of the Healing Christ, Emmet Fox died in France on August 13, 1951.

Herman Wolhorn once described Emmet Fox as "a man always gathering wisdom from every area of life." Dr. Fox once told his dear friend, "There is a lesson in everyone we meet." Indeed, Emmet Fox drew wisdom from all facets of life, from people, experiences, and publications.

We came to know and admire Emmet Fox through his writings, but we learned so much more about who he was through all of the great stories shared with us by the late Dr. Herman Wolhorn and his wife Blanche. (We have chronicled these stories in our book *Emmet Fox: His Life Story*.)

Even though Dr. Emmet Fox has passed into

that vibrant and potent silence, he still lives among us in the richest and fullest sense by those he has awakened to the new thought about man and the larger thought about God through his writings and teachings.

This book is a compilation of the private and confidential class notes of Dr. Fox which he presented in lecture form to his private metaphysical students. Dr. Herman Wolhorn handed down these important writings to us which have been archived for many years. It was Dr. Wolhorn's desire for this material to be published some years after his passing. He believed there would be a time when the teachings of Dr. Fox should be reintroduced, bringing back into the consciousness of people the wisdom of this remarkable New Thought teacher. This publication is fulfillment of that desire. We extend our sincere appreciation to Samuel Patrick Smith for his assistance in the preparation of this book.

Emmet Fox taught, "The vital thing in mental science is to practice it." These valuable notes, never before published in book form, give you the tools to practice the principles and to manifest your dreams.

Part One

Dr. Fox began this lesson with a meditation followed by a brief period of silence.

CLASS INTRODUCTION

We must begin our studies by getting a general knowledge of what life is. The object of this teaching is to enable you sooner or later to demonstrate Health, Prosperity and Happiness. In order to do this you must understand the meaning of life, you must know what man is, you must know what the universe is, and you must understand the Law of Life.

The first thing to realize is that there is simply no such thing as chance. Chance, luck, and hazard, do not exist. You are living in a universe of unbreakable unchangeable law, and if only you will realize what this means, every difficulty in your life will immediately assume a different aspect.

The fact that the Great Law exists can only mean that the difficulties and limitations in your life are there as the result of your fulfilling certain conditions, and from this it must follow that if you apply the laws differently these difficulties must disappear and harmony come to pass instead.

It is the appreciation of this reign of Law that marks the difference between bondage and freedom. As long as people suppose that sickness, trouble, and limitation have come to them by chance, or through the delinquency of some one else, they will naturally assume that their lives and happiness are at the mercy of other people. And, still worse, they will assume that health, prosperity and happiness can come to them as a matter of chance also. So we begin by realizing clearly that our lives, from the greatest events to the smallest details, are governed and conditioned by Law.

So far, so good. The next step now will obviously be to study the Law until we understand how conditions are created, and then by applying that understanding to ourselves and to our environment, gradually make our conditions whatever we wish them to be. Just as an understanding of the laws governing electricity enables the engineer to light our building, drive our railways, and generally adapt it to our service, so an intelligent understanding of the Law of Life sets us free.

The first thing you have to know is that in the entire universe there are only two things, namely Spirit and matter. It makes no difference if you go to the farthest star, you will only find two things, Spirit and matter. All the interactions of life are the interactions of these two. We shall therefore begin by considering the characteristic qualities of each.

First of all, Spirit is Divine. It is eternally perfect, has always existed, always will exist, and it cannot be hurt or damaged in any way. The spiritual world or spiritual plane is absolutely perfect; there nothing can ever go wrong, and so nothing ever needs to be healed or repaired or rearranged.

The other thing is matter, and the characteristics of matter are the precise contrary of those of Spirit. All material objects have a beginning and an end, they are always wearing out, always liable to decay, to damage, to wear and tear. Material objects never "stay put." They are here today, and gone tomorrow. "Of few days and full of trouble. Coming up as a flower to be cut down, fleeing as a shadow and continuing not." These two things are the fundamentals and are sometimes spoken of as Life and Form.

For practical purposes we shall find it convenient to divide the material world itself into two planes, the plane of invisible matter or ether, and the plane of visible, tangible or physical matter.

So now we are dealing with three planes, the Divine plane, which is Spirit, the etheric, or mental plane, which is the plane of thought, and the physical plane, which is the plane of manifestation.

There are various ways of considering man according to the purpose one has in view, but for our purpose as students of Practical Psychology and Metaphysics we shall follow the classifications made by St. Paul and divide man into three parts, to correspond to the three planes, namely, Body, Soul and Spirit. We shall not, however, employ the two latter English terms, as there is a good deal of ambiguity, especially in religious circles, concerning them. I shall, therefore, use instead the convenient Greek Testament terms, *Psyche* and *Pneuma*, as this renders any misunderstanding impossible. These are not three men—there is only one man—but at first we seem to have three things.

The body, of course is the ordinary physical body that we are familiar with. The thing that you see when you look in the glass. This is only the most intimate part of our physical embodiment and has been carefully studied and provided for by such sciences as physiology, hygiene, etc. The care of the body is very important, but nevertheless, as we shall find, secondary. You will see later that the whole of your environment, your home, your business, the neighborhood in which you live, etc., is really the embodiment of your psyche, and that what you call your body is only the nearest and most intimate part of this.

Next we come to *psyche*. Your psyche is your human mind, conscious and subconscious, and it constitutes your personality, the person that we know. It is actually made of ether, and consists indeed of an etheric vehicle somewhat larger than the physical body and interpenetrating it. It is your embodiment upon the etheric plane.

Now we come to Pneuma. Pneuma is your Real or Divine Self, the Spirit. The word Pneuma is, of course, the source of our familiar word pneumatic. Conventional psychology and religion speak, as a rule, of the body and soul only, but this is a deadly error and the reason why the world has not made much greater progress throughout the ages. It is not until you get the three-fold division that you have the truth concerning man. Pneuma is your Real Self, the real you. The Ego. Each of us has this Real Self behind the psyche. It is the Divine part of us. Call it your Higher Self, or your Real Self, or the Divine Spark, what you please, it is there, and it never gets ill, or tired or angry. It was never born, it has existed from all eternity, and it will never die. It has never made any mistakes, and knows neither fear nor anxiety. It is always in full communion with the Divine. It is what makes us men and women and not animals. It is what people really refer to when they speak of the Inner Light. We, our real selves, are not evolved animals, and the Divine is always present within to heal us and teach us. It is only when you come to Pneuma that you touch the Miracle.

In this class we are giving our attention principally to the psyche, and we must now consider in some detail what the characteristics and powers of the psyche are. We are indeed wonderfully made, and only the consideration of the almost unlimited powers and potentialities of the human psyche will enable us to realize what glorious and thrilling destiny is ours.

The psyche exists in two great parts or divisions, usually called the *conscious mind* and the *subconscious mind*, though some psychologists prefer to call the conscious the *objective*, and the subconscious the *subjective*. Until quite recently most people were totally unaware of the existence of the subconscious mind, but this long neglect is now being compensated for by the extraordinary amount of attention it is receiving today. What most people had been in the habit of calling their "mind" that is the conscious mind, turns out to be only a very small part of the whole psyche. By far the greater proportion is subconscious, or unconscious, or not consciously known to ourselves. We do not know what is going on there, but all sorts of interesting and important things are going on, and it expresses the fact well to say that about 97 percent of the psyche is subconscious, and only about three percent conscious.

TREATMENT

The application of these principles to a practical problem is called treatment. The simplest form of Spiritual Treatment is this. When you are in any difficulty, stop thinking of the trouble and identify with Pneuma instead. Withdraw your attention from yourself, the physical and mental planes and concentrate on the spiritual.

Then deny that the trouble exists on the Spiritual Plane, repeating the denial as many times as you feel to be necessary.

Then go on to affirm as many good and harmonious things as you can think of about Pneuma. Any good that you can think of must be true about Pneuma, who expresses perfect and complete harmony.

You will see that this is really the Golden Key, plus the denial.

CONSCIOUS AND SUBCONSCIOUS MIND

It is necessary for the student to distinguish carefully between the respective functions of the conscious and the subconscious minds. Each has its own work to do and neither can perform the work of the other. It is to this arrangement that we owe our free will. In no other way would it be possible for men to have freedom of choice and at the same time to reap, as he does, only the results of his own sowing.

To begin with the conscious mind we note that it possesses the faculty of inductive reasoning or what we roughly call "common sense." This is the great prerogative of the conscious mind. We may also note that it has quite a limited field of attention, as distinguished from the subconscious mind whose field appears to be unlimited, and that in itself it possesses very little strength.

It informs itself of the physical world by means of the five senses, and it has the power of impressing all sorts of suggestions, good and bad, upon the subconscious mind. And in fact, one might say that it is the throne of the I AM.

25

The subconscious mind, on the other hand, has a different role altogether. First and foremost it builds and rebuilds the body constantly, in accordance with the pattern or mind model that it possesses. As we shall see, it exercises no discretion in this matter, but taking the pattern for granted, builds the physical body in accordance therewith.

It also governs all such functions as breathing, digestion, the circulation, the elimination, and so on.

It has been well described by one of our leading scientists as a super-chemist, for it makes itself responsible for both the quantity and the nature of all bodily secretions. And it can actually produce anything required for the welfare of the body.

The next point to note about the subconscious is that it seems to have unlimited strength or power.

One reason why we sometimes find it so difficult to manage ourselves, for instance, to break a bad habit such as smoking, or lying too long in bed, is owing to this tremendous strength of the subconscious. Not knowing how to work, people push in one direction with the feeble strength of the conscious, while the immense power of the subconscious is pushing in the opposite direction, and so they fail.

The subconscious mind has a perfect memory. Everything that has ever occurred to you, everything you have ever seen, or heard, or read, even the things which you did not take conscious notice of at the time, such as the people you passed in the street, things your eyes have seen in shop windows, and so on, are all correctly recorded in your subconscious mind, and nothing but spiritual treatment can wipe one of these records out. Hypnotism or suggestion will sometimes push these records out of sight, as it were, by kind of counter-pressure, but this does not eliminate them. Only spiritual treatment will do that. This perfect record is what is really meant by the "Judgment Books" of Scripture. Authentic cases are on record of people who have been almost drowned, who tell us that, in a flash as it seemed, the entire record unrolled before them, and their whole past lives were seen.

The subconscious has perfect and unlimited power of deductive reasoning. This means that given any premise it will work out the natural sequence with infallible logic, a thing that the conscious mind very seldom does.

Finally, the subconscious is always tending to express or reproduce on the physical plane every idea that has been presented to it. That is to say, every idea, which enters the subconscious, is, in a manner of speaking, accepted by it as an order to be carried out; and at the first possible opportunity it will present you with the idea in the concrete form of an accomplished fact.

We can easily see, now, how important it is to be careful what ideas we allow to enter our subconscious. The subconscious does not use any discretion, but taking everything it gets to be an order, seeks to bring it into our lives at the earliest possible moment. This is why one should avoid as far as possible reading detailed accounts of diseases, crimes, and all sorts of unpleasant happenings. This is also the reason why, to hold evil thoughts about other people is so damaging for ourselves. The evil thought, as such, is accepted at its face value. Going into the subconscious it is taken for an order, and the tendency there is for it to be worked out in one's life as soon as possible.

The Science of Living

Many people at the present day who understand this process are not so clear upon the other point, namely the power of unlimited deductive reasoning possessed by the subconscious.

Our conscious minds have so little power of deduction that it is usually limited to drawing the most obvious conclusions, and to a little simple mental arithmetic. The subconscious, however, immediately works out to finality the ultimate logical conclusion of any idea presented to it, and the ultimate logical conclusion of many ideas, harmless looking enough in themselves, is often something extremely unpleasant. Nevertheless, it will make its appearance in concrete form on the physical plane when the circumstances are favorable. People often say, for instance, that some difficulty, perhaps a physical malady, has come into their lives though they had never thought of it. The explanation is that while they did not, indeed, think of this particular thing, they did think of things, or they did hold beliefs, which, in their logical outcome could only culminate in the materialization of that particular trouble.

It is now much easier to see why we have to be constantly on our guard to think only thoughts of harmony peace, and goodwill; for the logical outcome of such thinking is health, happiness and prosperity; while the logical outcome of criticism, spite, self-pity, etc., is sickness, poverty and limitation.

RACE MIND

As we look about us we seem to be quite separate people, but this is an illusion. It is true that our bodies are separate, but our subconscious minds are all joined together by the common human race mind. And so the human race is really one. Just as the fingers of the hand are all joined together in the palm, so all individual subconscious minds are joined together in the race mind. In other words we are all really limbs of one body, and this is why telepathy is possible, why it is possible for an individual to draw upon the general store of race knowledge; and incidentally, why selfishness is always such a bad policy, for when we injure someone else we really injure ourselves. The old world comparison to an archipelago is still very apt. Each island seems to be quite separate, but we know that they are all really joined up under the sea, so that, theoretically, one could sink a shaft in one island, tunnel under the bed of the ocean, and come up through a similar shaft in another island. This corresponds to what takes place in telepathy.

The conscious mind corresponds to that part of the island above water, the individual subconscious mind to the part of the island under water (usually a submerged mountain) and the main body of the earth to the race mind. Another way of looking at it is to say that your subconscious is your own individual apportionment of the race mind.

You will now see why your mind is always more or less subject to the incursion of ideas and thoughts from the general race mind, and why it is necessary for you to be on your guard in this respect.

Actually nothing can enter your individual mentality from the race mind unless it is something that you are attuned for. By "treating" ourselves constantly for such things as understanding, wisdom, purity and so on, we make it more and more difficult for undesirable race thoughts to tune in, until at last it will be impossible for certain thoughts to affect us at all, when we can say, "The prince of this world cometh and findeth nothing in me."

Treat yourself by affirming quietly that you are Pneuma and possess these things now.

For certain purposes you will find it very helpful to think of your individual mentality as being a wireless set which is certain to receive exactly the program for which it is tuned, and no other. In this case you tune yourself out of an undesirable program and into a good one by treatment.

It is from the common race mind that we get all the ideas and beliefs that we, as a race, have in common. The race mind thinks limitation of all kinds, but it never thinks that any one must have disease or trouble; this is why it is so very much easier to heal than to overcome limitation.

HEALING

In this teaching we use the word healing in a much more general sense than is usual. We speak of healing business affairs, and apply the word also to such things as the settling of a quarrel, a lawsuit, and so on. From what has been said about the subconscious mind you will now realize that what is commonly called the body is really only the most intimate part of your embodiment. Your psyche has certain qualities, faculties and beliefs, and that psyche has to be embodied. The whole of your environment, your physical body, your home, your business place, the people with whom you mix, those whom you dislike as well as those you like, are but the outer embodiment of your own mentality. Most people have been in the habit of looking upon all these things as quite independent of themselves, but you now understand that every condition in your life, good or bad, you have drawn to yourself by your own thinking. The Law of Attraction which is another way of stating the law of Karma, has drawn these people to you: those friends, that employer, that husband or wife, that home, that trade or profession, and so on.

For the moment we will concern ourselves with the healing of the physical body.

The first point to know is that your body is quite constantly being renewed by nature. This is made possible owing to the fact that our bodies are built on the unit principle, the principle upon which so many modern machines are built. That means that it is an assemblage of separate parts. If a certain part of a good typewriter, for instance, becomes damaged, it is a simple matter to remove it and replace it with a similar part, which is certain to fit exactly. This is the unit system. And nature has designed us in just the same way, and for just the same reason, that as soon as any part wears out it can be replaced, if only we will let it. The separate units of which the body is built are called cells. We are really composed of an enormous number of little separate cells, and these cells are being constantly renewed. Some are renewed much more often than others, but it is estimated that the entire body is renewed about once every twelve months. That is to say, it is literally true to affirm that no body in the world is much more than twelve months old. This is quite apparent in the case of the hair and the nails, which grow visibly, and in the case of the outer skin, which rubs off, but is equally true about every part of the body. The rate of change varies between one organ and another, the bones for instance, changing more slowly. Again, some people renew everything more slowly than others. About twelve months is a good average. Nature actually intends a complete renewal every nine months which is the natural cycle, but owing to subconscious fear, race habit, and so on, it is somewhat slowed down in practice.

The student will naturally inquire why, if he gets a new body about every year, the new one is so like the old, and the answer is simple.

It used to be thought by many people that a new cell simply copied its predecessor, but this is not correct. If it were there would be no healing at all, since, as the new cells grew, they would simply copy the old tissue. What actually happens is this. In your subconscious you have a pattern human body. As the new cells arrive they must conform to this pattern; they do not copy each his predecessor, but conform to the pattern or model in the subconscious mind of the individual. Now if you want to know what kind of subconscious model you possess, well, look in the glass, or get a medical examination, because your present physical body is the perfect embodiment of your subconscious body-model or design.

Just as a building or a ship is the embodiment of certain drawings, specifications, and blueprints in the office of the architect or builder, so your body is the expression of your subconscious blueprint.

Before a building is erected the architect prepares precise drawings of exactly what he wants produced. These drawings are then handed over to the builder, and the builder embodies them in stone, brick, steel and so on. Of course the architect does not put in the blueprint anything he does not want in the finished building, nor does he expect to find in the building anything which he has omitted to put in the drawings. After the building is finished a complete set of drawings is always retained in the archives of the firm which built it, and should it be necessary to rebuild any part of the finished edifice, owing to wear and tear, or perhaps in consequence of an accident, it can always be done quite easily by reference to the drawings.

Now this forms a perfect analogy with the human subject. Your drawing or blueprint is the subconscious body-model that you hold. The application of the parable is very obvious. If you are dissatisfied with the state of your body, that is to say if your are not in the enjoyment of perfect health, the thing to do is to change your subconscious model. Until you do so, the body cannot change. The subconscious is your obedient servant who will not fail to build according to the drawing that you provide. It will use no discretion in this matter, any more than a foreman builder would dare to depart from the blueprint provided by the architect. You are the architect of your own fortunes in this matter, as in all others. It is for you to choose whether you will have health or ill health, beauty or ugliness, the joy of life or invalidism, in accordance with the kind of model that you present to your faithful master-builder.

The first step therefore in self-healing is to start to substitute a perfect model for the imperfect one.

An excellent form of treatment is that already given. If you can realize Pneuma clearly enough it will heal anything. Every time you get any realization of the Spiritual Plane, and especially the Pneuma, your whole psyche including your body-model improves automatically.

In addition to this form, however, you must learn to "Speak the Word," which is much quicker and better adapted for most ordinary purposes. If for example you are feeling unwell, or you have cut yourself, or have an attack of indigestion, simply tell Psyche quietly to put it right. Say, "Heal this" or "Put this right." It may be necessary, in the beginning to repeat the order a number of times, but later this will not be necessary. In the same way you should train your psyche to get you up at whatever time in the morning that you order overnight, to remind you to do certain things at a later hour in the day, and so on. You do not need any knowledge of physiology or therapeutics for this. Simply say, "You know what needs to be done; do it."

When treating yourself in this manner never speak in a singsong way as in so-called autosuggestion, but give your orders in a rational way as in addressing and intelligent servant.

"Thou shalt decree a thing, and it shall be established unto thee."

Read up to the history of Jesus and the fig tree (Mark 11:12) and note the warning about the necessity of forgiving everyone before you employ the Power of the Word. Otherwise the power is so great that it will injure yourself.

Before you go to sleep at night you can say, "I shall have a quiet refreshing sleep and wake at such an hour feeling well and happy. All day tomorrow I shall be peaceful and happy. I shall do my work well and quickly."

If you find any difficulty in rising in the morning say, "I shall be up and dressing at such a time." Decree the thing you actually want.

THE LAW OF REVERSED EFFORT

Some people find at first that things get a little worse when they speak the word. For instance, speaking the word overnight results in a disturbed sleep. This is by no means the rule, but it does occur, and is due to what is called the Law of Reversed Effort. The remedy is simply to persevere, when matters will come right. It is worthwhile having a few disturbed nights to acquire the Power of the Word. A few nights, or a week or two at the outside, will see you through.

FREE WILL

You have free will. To know this is the beginning of everything. People continue in difficulties because they do not really believe they have free will, or they would seek to overcome them. It is necessary, however, to understand exactly in what free will consists. You must realize that it does not mean omnipotence. It means, really, that you have freedom of choice within certain limits, and subject to certain conditions. For example, a person who cannot play the piano has not free will to sit down and play a difficult piece forthwith. His free will consists in the ability to play a piece after certain appropriate steps have been taken, what we call learning to play the piano, and this always involves a time lag. In the same way, in certain cases of healing it is found that a certain process of time enters in.

Our free will lies in our choice of thoughts. Once the thoughts have been entertained the natural consequences on the physical plane must follow, unless of course they are overtaken and wiped out by treatment. This brings us to the important point that cause-and-effect lies between a thought, or sequence of thoughts, on the mental plane and the physical manifestation; not, as is generally supposed, between one physical manifestation and another. That is to say, your outer conditions at any moment are the result of your mental condition at that moment, and not of any previous outer conditions.

THE LAW

Now we come to the consideration of the Law. A great deal is heard of the Law but many people lack a definite understanding of what it really means. Briefly, the Law is this: there is an unbreakable sequence of cause and effect right throughout the universe. This sequence is never broken, and therefore there is no such thing as favoritism, special providences, hard cases, or anything of that sort. As we sow we reap. Every deed results in certain consequences, and these consequences come to us as the result of the deed, and that is all about it. This is the Law, and once we understand this we have taken the first great step on the road to freedom. We then understand that if we do not desire certain consequences to come into our lives, we must not set them going by taking the corresponding action. If we do not want the goods delivered we must not order them.

In past time it was only the more developed souls, the great Initiates, who were able to grasp this principle, but now, in these days of general education and general understanding of natural science, the "man in the street" thoroughly understands the idea of law. He quite understands that if the electric light will not work, or if the wireless is dumb, it is simply because the laws of electricity have been transgressed, not because some mysterious power has a "down" on him, or because someone is trying to punish him. He knows that because the laws of electricity have been transgressed he will get no light or sound, as the case may be, but for the same reason he also knows that as soon as the law has been fulfilled (by the putting in of a fuse or the closing of a switch or whatever may be required) then nothing whatever can prevent his getting his light or his music. Now we have reached the point when we understand that this idea of law is not confined to electricity, chemistry, or mechanics, but runs through the entire gamut of human experience. Every difficulty in our lives, from a petty annoyance to a broken heart comes under the Law, just as surely as does our electric light, our wireless set, or our motorcar.

The first consequence to us of appreciating this tremendous truth is that when we find ourselves in difficulties we do not blame other people. This of course is usually the first impulse, but it is a fatal one. If you do not look for the trouble in the right place you cannot locate it and put it right. If the bedroom light goes out, it is no use tampering with the scullery fuse. In the same way, since all our troubles are due to our own mistakes and we cannot by any chance suffer for anybody else's mistakes, to blame other people when things go wrong is simply to try to repair the wrong fuse.

If we sow right thoughts and actions, health, prosperity and happiness must come into our lives, irrespective of what anyone else may think or do. If we sow wrong or foolish thoughts or deeds, then trouble must come sooner or later somewhere, sometime, somehow, irrespective of what anyone else may do.

This Law is known in the East as the Law of

Karma. To many people this term covers a great mystery. But really there is nothing magical or mystical about it.

The Law of Karma is simply the Law of Cause and Effect. Now notice particularly that this is not fatalism. Most people who acquire a superficial knowledge of the Law do jump to the conclusion that it means fatalism, that "what is to be, will be," and that all one can do is to sit down and take what is coming to him, with as good a grace as possible. This however is not Karma at all; this is *kismet*, a very different thing. The Mohammedan believes that his destiny is already settled; "written upon his forehead" is their expression. We should probably say that his life is a play that is already written, and that he has but to act a part. Just as, let us say, an actress who is playing the role of Desdemona somewhere tonight, knows now that she will start in a Venetian Palace soon after eight o'clock this evening, and that she will be strangled in due form about twenty minutes past ten. That is kismet, not Karma.

The Law says that certain consequences will follow to you from certain thoughts and actions, but it also says that you can choose your thoughts and your acts and thereby order the kind of consequences that you want to bring into your life, and that you can do this at any time. It matters not how great may be your difficulties at the moment, the Law says that just because you have brought these difficulties upon yourself by the wrong thoughts or deeds of the past, so now by starting to think and act wisely, and by persisting in so doing, all your difficulties must disappear sooner or later, and perfect harmony be yours.

The beginner would do well to give a good deal of consideration to this subject. He should meditate upon the Law of Karma frequently until he is satisfied that he really understands it. Those who dread to think about it are those who fear it because they do not understand it. The better you understand it the more joy will you have in contemplating it. It takes all the sting out of trouble, and it opens the door to freedom and self-expression. It really does "justify the ways of God to man."

People are fond of quoting the poem of Burroughs which says, "My own shall come to me," but I find in most cases that they do not understand what Burroughs meant. The well

45

known lines say:

> "Nor time nor space nor height nor depth
> Shall keep my own away from me,"

and they think that this means that if only
they will sit down with their hands folded, and
wait patiently, that sometime or other some-
body or other, perhaps a fairy or an angel, will
come along and present them with all the things
they want in life, all ready made. These good
people sit down waiting year after year, but
nothing ever happens to them, and, of course,
nothing ever will, except that they get a little
older, a little poorer, a little more depressed.

The meaning of the line is this: Not that your
own will come to you in a mysterious way at
some future time, but that your own is always
coming to you everywhere, at all times. Because
the Law is what it is, every one of us is at all
times getting exactly what belongs to him. This
means that at any given moment you are always
exactly where you belong at that moment. It
means that no matter how much you may be
suffering, no matter how unhappy you may be,
the fact remains that because you are at the
moment the person that you are, nothing else

could possibly happen to you, and therefore, unpleasant as things may be, you really are in your right place.

But let me hasten to add that although you must be in your right place at the moment, there is no reason whatever why you should remain there a single day longer, if you do not wish to. The person that you are now could not be anywhere else, but if only you will make yourself a different person, then because you have become a different person you must inevitably move out of the position of dislike. Make yourself even slightly different, and that place will no longer belong to you, and what does not belong to you, you must, of course, lose. This briefly is what we mean by the Law.

Beginners seldom get a good understanding of it easily. You will need to read over this chapter a number of times and reflect a good deal upon it before you grasp it thoroughly. Make a point of doing this, because a partial knowledge of the Law is rather dangerous. As we have seen it leads to fatalism, and fatalism is the end of everything. If you think that either good things or bad things must inevitably come to you, you will make no attempt to put the Law in motion for yourself, and that means that you will never get anywhere.

OUTLINING

Never treat for a particular appointment, a particular house, a particular partner, or any particular solution of your difficulty. This is technically called "outlining" and is always wrong. You never really know what is best for the future although you may think you do. Leave the question of ways and means to Divine Wisdom. Treat for the right house, or position, or whatever it is you want, and if the particular one you have in mind is the right one, you will get it; if not you will get something better.

In the healing of the body there is no danger of outlining, as there is a standard human body.

A GENERAL FORM OF TREATMENT

The student is now in a position to appreciate the rationale of treatment. The physical plane being only the embodiment of thoughts and beliefs on the mental plane, and having no character of its own, any of its conditions can be healed or adjusted by mental or spiritual treatment.

Get by yourself at a time when you can be sure of not being disturbed for at least half an hour. You may not really require more than five or ten minutes but you must be able to feel that you can have half-an-hour if necessary.

Read the Bible, or Emerson, or any book that appeals to you, until you feel that you have gotten away somewhat from the everyday things.

Then close the book, and be quiet for a moment (be sure not to get tense or nervous).

Then say, "I am Pneuma; Divine Spirit, I have Dominion in His name. I want (the right position or employment; the right house, the necessary money, etc.)."

Then say, "I know that Divine Wisdom will send this in some good way."

Then dismiss all thought of the matter until the next treatment.

As a rule it is inadvisable to treat more than once a day. If the thing keeps coming up, quietly give thanks for the accomplished demonstration: this thanksgiving is itself a very powerful treatment.

You do not require great faith in the sense of

optimism. If you have enough faith to give the treatment, that will be enough. This is the grain of mustard seed.

An obstinate case may take time. The thing is to keep on treating, and the demonstration must come.

INSPIRATION AND GUIDANCE

For inspiration for creative work or for guidance for a specific problem, proceed in exactly the same way, claiming a new idea, or the best way out of your difficulty, instead of a house or a position.

The answer will usually come in the course of a day or two, and when you are not thinking about the subject. It may come in the form of a sudden thought, or you may open a book seemingly at random and find what you want, or you may meet someone who helps you, or practically anything may happen.

EXTERNAL REORGANIZATION

An important part of the redemption or re-education of your subconscious will consist in the reorganization of your general daily life on scientific or businesslike lines. This means that you must arrange your personal habits, methods of working, etc., to secure the highest degree of efficiency possible for you at the moment. As a result of this policy you will not only reap the immediate benefit of a freer, happier, fuller, and much healthier, and more prosperous life, but this policy will, in itself bring about far-reaching changes in the subconscious, enabling you as time goes on to obtain without very great difficulty demonstrations which might otherwise be almost impossible for you.

Begin by having a general stocktaking of your life. Do not carry this out in any spirit of morbid introspection. The task is really one of looking outward toward your daily activities, rather than within yourself. Look at your own daily life, but as if you were inspecting someone else's activities. Make a written list of the things that obviously need to be altered immediately. Do not be fussy in this. Do not waste time blaming yourself for defects, but get to work vigorously now, and repair them. Do not be afraid to laugh at yourself; this is a very good sign.

After your stocktaking is completed, the next step in most cases is to arrange for yourself something like a Standard Day. This is on no account to become a hard and fast rule, which may not be broken, but, nevertheless, it should be there as a standard to be adhered to, except whenever there is good reason for departing from it. Of course the standard day will hardly be the same for any two people, because conditions of life vary so much. The employer and the employee, the businessman and the housewife, the countryman and the townsman will all have very different needs in this respect, but all can form a standard. Students and schoolchildren will find such a standard particularly helpful. Record your standard in the form of a written schedule. This need not be at all elaborate; a half sheet of note paper will suffice in many cases, but get it into writing. Then as you go on you will find that you will need to make alterations in your schedule from time to time, as experience dictates. Do not hesitate to do this. The schedule must never become a sacred rule, a superstition, but simply a matter of personal convenience and efficiency. You will never hesitate to depart from it whenever there is any good reason. When you are away from home, for example, you will necessarily vary it in certain respects, or under the call of duty in any form, but it is surprising how closely one can keep to a chosen routine in even unfamiliar surroundings, when one chooses.

Of course you will always cheerfully cancel your arrangements to help another, when you really can help them, but do not allow people to waste your time.

The details of the schedule are what will constitute its usefulness. In this matter you must make the fullest use of the Cosmic Principle of Rhythm. All natural motion is found to be rhythmical, from the (to us) inconceivably rapid vibrations of atoms and molecules to the stately swing of the planets in their orbits. Nature works in regular rhythmical cycles or periods. The coming and going of the seasons in regular order, and the regular rise and fall of the tides are examples of the universal Cosmic Law of Rhythm. The mechanism and growth of the human body, both male and female, is no exception to this rule. It functions best in regular periodicity. It will always be a little easier, often much easier, to do a thing, when you have already done it several times before at the same time of day, or in the same sequence relative to other things.

For this reason you should form as many good habits as possible. By doing a thing voluntarily a number of times it will presently become a habit to do it without taking much conscious thought, so that it is almost automatic. The valuable result of this is to save both your time and energy for other things.

Make a list of the things that you must do every day, and see if you cannot make an improvement in the order in which you do them, or in the mode of doing the things themselves. You know, for example, that you have to rise, shave, bathe, read personal letters, and the newspaper, answer personal correspondence, and so on.

Have a fixed time for rising in the morning and retiring at night, and keep to it, except where there is a really good reason for departure. Occasionally, for instance, when there is some special work to be finished, it may be wise to remain up much later, but do not sit up beyond your schedule time just to finish an interesting book.

Make a list of useful habits that you wish to acquire, and check your progress by constant reference to your list. You could glance through it each evening, noting how far you have fallen short during that day. If there is any particular mental or spiritual quality, for instance, that you desire to possess, note it down, treat regularly for it, and check your progress in the same way.

Keep a notebook and refer to it constantly. Jot down every good idea that comes to you, or that you hear, or read of. Unless you reread your notes frequently they will be of very little use. Put down ideas for future work, useful information of all kinds, and so on.

Keep a notebook and pencil near your bed and enter in abbreviated form any good idea that comes, especially in the morning.

Before you start a particular task you should know, broadly, what it is you are going to do. Nothing distinguishes the amateur from the competent worker more than this. Inexperienced people waste a great deal of time in blind groping and vagueness. Have a definite plan. It is not spiritual to be vague or to muddle along indefinitely. When possible have the general program of work for each day sketched out the day before, or earlier.

Do not waste time. Do not digress in your work. Do not allow other people to waste your time.

Have a special drawer or basket and label it Work Waiting. Put in here all letters that for any reason you cannot answer at once, and all matter that needs attention, unfinished work of any kind; and put nothing else in this receptacle. This will prevent urgent things from being overlooked and save you from getting into arrears. You can then always tell at a glance what needs to be done.

"Order is Heaven's first Law." You must have order in material things. This is quite fundamental. All your possessions, books, papers, household goods of every description must be arranged in good order. A place for everything, and everything in its place. If you cannot keep things tidy, get rid of them.

Do not hold on to things that you do not want. Many people are hoarding all sorts of rubbish that should be either in the dustbin or given away to someone who could make use of it. Many men have one or two suits put away that they will never wear again. People keep stacks of old letters, pamphlets, books, music, anything, because they cannot make up their minds to part with them. All such junk should be ruthlessly thrown out. Pay someone to take it away. Do not keep a thing for years "because it may come in handy some day." It probably never will, but in any case it is better to buy it new when the time comes, than to be burdened with it in the meantime. Clear the decks.

Always keep abreast of your work. Never allow it to get into arrears. If such a thing happens, sit up all night if necessary until you clear up and get square again. It will be difficult for inspiration to come through if the sense of arrears of work is weighing on your mind.

PROMPT DECISION

You must form the power of quick decision. Nothing is more detrimental than the habit of vacillation and indecision. You can train yourself to make rapid and wise decisions in this way. Begin immediately in all the ordinary affairs of life where a decision is called for, to make a "snap" decision. Decide in whichever way comes to you first. And having taken your decision adhere to it. Do not be tempted to reverse or revise it on second thoughts. It is very probable that for a few days, or even a week or two, you will make mistakes which could have been avoided by following second thoughts, but you must put up with this inconvenience for a short time. It is well worth it for the subsequent benefit that you will derive. Presently you will find that your quick decision will be the right one ninety-nine times in a hundred and much sounder than the opinion you would have formed after labored reflection.

It would not usually be advisable to come to a very momentous decision in this way, in the beginning, until you have acquired experience, but proceed in this way for all but the most important things. Later you will use it with confidence for everything.

DIET

It is not well to insist on uniformity in this matter. There is no such thing as a "best" diet for everyone, because nothing in the world is so individual. One man's "meat" is indeed another man's "poison." You must find out by experiment what diet suits you best, making intelligent allowance for the summer and winter seasons, and for different climates when away from home, etc.

A book on diet may furnish rules and menus that are excellent for conditions of life in one country, which is perhaps warm and dry and yet be quite unsuitable for the damp cold climate of Britain. Experiment until you find what suits you best.

There are however, three general principles, which might be called the Three Golden Rules. They were taught years ago by the late Horace Fletcher. They are:

(1) Never eat until you are really hungry. Do not eat just because it is one o'clock, or because the family is having a meal. If you have any doubts as to whether you are hungry or not, you are not. A false appetite often presents itself, which means that you are not really hungry although you think you are. This is to be detected by having a drink of water. If the appetite is a false one it will then disappear. If it does not disappear, then have your meal and enjoy it. By forming regular habits of eating these

sort of doubts will disappear.

(2) Chew every mouthful of food very thoroughly, extracting the entire flavor from it. The tendency with many people is to bolt every bite in order to get at the next one. They never really enjoy anything they eat, and derive comparatively little benefit from their food.

(3) Never eat when you are angry, or in a state of fear, nor indulge in critical thoughts during a meal. If any of these states of mind overtakes you treat yourself until you are free, and then eat.

The observance of these rules will alone overcome many digestive difficulties, and will gradually train the psyche to guide you aright in the selection of food itself.

ELIMINATION

Nothing is more important for the health of the body than efficient elimination. Inner cleanliness is, if possible, even more important than outer cleanliness. Habit is very important here. Give the bowels an opportunity to act at about the same time every day, preferably in the morning.

AIR

Of course you will see to it that you have open windows and plenty of fresh air wherever you are, especially in the sleeping apartment.

EXERCISES

A few simple physical exercises done daily without any apparatus will be found of great benefit by all. Especially the bending and stretching movements. The action should not be jerky, but rhythmical and of a sweeping nature. Those with any physical disability should only do physical exercises under medical advice.

PROSPERITY

Now we come to the question of money, or supply. The first thing that you have to know is why you should treat for money at all, and why it is right to wish to be prosperous, because up to the present this has not been a part of orthodox religion. We have been accustomed to think that although we ought to pray for help in times of temptation, and when we are ill, we ought not to pray for money unless we are in dire straits. If a man were at the very end of his resources and on the point of being turned out of his home everybody would say that it was his duty to pray for help, and that if he did so in the right spirit God would surely help him. Every orthodox person would say that this was the right thing to do. But the truth is that, instead of waiting for the emergency to arise, it is much more sensible to treat regularly for supply so that hard times may never come, and that is what you must do.

The real object in demonstrating supply is this, that as long as you are pressed for money you cannot really think about anything else. As long as you do not know where the rent is coming from, and particularly if you have others dependent on you, that problem will monopolize every bit of your attention.

But the only thing in life that is really worth doing is to get a better knowledge of Truth, that is, to develop your soul, and it is certain that you cannot do this if your attention is preoccupied with something else. So money is necessary and the Divine Power provides everything that is necessary for us.

The Science of Living

God provides everything in abundance, and so has provided abundance for you. But what is abundance? Abundance means that you have such an amount of money in your possession that you never have to think about money. That is abundance, and nothing less, and nothing more than that can be called abundance. If you have to scheme to make ends meet, or if you have to spend much time and attention on looking after your possessions because they are so vast, then you are a slave to them, and you cannot be said to have established harmony in financial matters. You must have enough money to be independent. You must not make money into a god or into a devil. You must never feel, "I should like to do that, but I cannot afford it." You must be able to organize your life as you wish to live it, without reference to money at all. That is the freedom of the children of God. When you are in this teaching your life will have a purpose and a meaning, and money will come into your life only to bring happiness. Money never brings trouble upon people when it comes through treatment; it is a blessing to all concerned.

The word "supply" is often used instead of

money, because what we really want is not money, as such, but clothing, books, food, houses, railway fares, etc. Nevertheless, in civilized countries it is nearly always easier for these things to come to us through the medium of money, and so money is what one usually gets through treatment.

You can get all the money you want for any wise purpose through treatment. There is no need for anyone who knows how to treat to be in money difficulties. But you must treat. As in all other cases there is no substitute for treatment. Merely talking about treatment, or vague dreaming or pious resolutions will get you nowhere. Treat, and poverty must go.

The first thing necessary, is that you should be genuinely convinced that it is the Divine will for you to have all that you need. If you have any lingering doubts on this point they will make it difficult for you to demonstrate, and in that case you must begin by treating for wisdom. There's no good in poverty. What is called "voluntary poverty" is not poverty at all. Real poverty is simply limitation. Poverty has spoiled so many lives it is not usually a difficult thing to handle, because there is no great sub-

The Science of Living

conscious terror underlying it, as in the case of many physical diseases.

It is really a bad habit. It is the result of thinking poverty thoughts continually. Change your thinking, and the poverty goes. As long as you think poverty, you will be poor; think abundance and abundance will come; slowly at first, perhaps, but with a rapid rate of increase. Notice that people who have once made money do not as a rule have much difficulty, should they lose it, in making it again. Prosperity is a habit. People who have always been in poverty usually remain poor to the end of their days, for the same reason.

You must never outline any particular source from which the money will come. That is the greatest, and unfortunately, the most frequent mistake made. People treat that someone will buy some jewelry that they possess, or perhaps a house or a farm. This is wrong and only delays the demonstration. If you want money, treat for money, and leave the mode of demonstration to God. If you want to get rid of a house or a jewel, that is a different thing. Treat for that, and the right thing will happen; but if you want money treat for money and leave the source absolutely open.

You have nothing to deal with but your own psyche. Get this right and the money will come. It is not enough to treat for money if you want to be consistently prosperous; you must keep your thoughts right on the subject all day long. Above all you must never want to get something for nothing, nor be willing to accept it either. A present is a different matter; it is a definite expression of love with its own place in the scheme of things, but that does not concern us here. You must give up running to sales, for instance. You must not want anything "on the cheap." You must be desirous of paying the shopkeeper a just price for what you buy. Go to a good shop and pay the right price for a good article. If you have not the money, then treat for supply. When some people enter a theatre you hear them say at the box-office, "Is that the cheapest seat you have?" That is to stamp yourself with the brand of poverty. When you go to the theatre get a good seat where you can see the show well and be comfortable; if you have not the money for that, stay at home and treat for supply.

If anyone does work for you you must pay

them the proper rate of pay. You must refuse to countenance undercutting.

Do not allow other people to cut you down. You will never help people by giving them something for nothing. That stamps them with the poverty consciousness.

It is seldom good to give people money, although there will be rare exceptions. A treatment will do far more for them.

Never buy an article of poor quality or make. Go without it until you can demonstrate the proper price. You need not buy "deluxe" objects, but what you possess must be good of its kind.

If you wish to prosper it is absolutely necessary that you should do your day's work, whatever it is, to the very best of you ability. There must be no slackness or inefficiency. If you are an employee and your employer is not treating you fairly, do your duties as well as you can, and treat. Then, either the employer will change for the better, or you will find yourself in another situation.

If you are selling goods you must make sure that they are good in quality, and that they come up to the description in all respects. If this is the case then treatment will increase your sales indefinitely. But you must not try to sell a poor article.

You must never try to persuade people to buy against their inclinations. If a man orders something and you have reason to think that he would like to alter his mind, you should at once release him.

If you are out of employment, treat and accept the first job that offers. There must be no question of being too proud to do any kind of honest work. Take what offers and treat for something better if it is not to your liking. Often this is the way the path opens. If you are already in a position do not change until you find something better. Continue treating.

Some people ask whether it is right to accumulate money in the bank. Yes, you would not go out without money in the morning and trust to a treatment to materialize it at the railway station. You would not try to materialize the price of your lunch while the waiter was serving you. If you are not satisfied about the investment of your money, if you think you may not be putting it to good use, treat for guidance.

The Science of Living

It is better to insure your house against fire than to waste time treating against fire every day. Better devote that time to healing the sick.

If you have only three-half pence in the world, you can make a good beginning by spending that three-halfpence like a gentleman, that is, by not trying to get two pennyworth for it.

A "large sum" is only whatever you think large. A millionaire would have no difficulty in demonstrating thousands of pounds by treatment. A laborer would find it impossible, but could begin with a pound or two. This would build up his faith, and gradually he could acquire riches.

Do not outline where the money is coming from.

Where money has to come in by a definite date there will be more or less acute fear present; concentrate on getting rid of the fear, and when it is gone you will have the money. Realize that Pneuma knows nothing but Divine Love, and try to get away from all thoughts of money, debts, etc. If you can do this for a very few moments fear will go and you will demonstrate. But do not think that you are not doing good work because you are not getting a realization. All the time you are working you are getting nearer to freedom. Keep on.

To get promotion in business realize that Pneuma is always in his right place. What is his place? His place is the ideas of which he is conscious at any time. Do not sit down and wait for dead men's shoes. Your real self (Pneuma) is always conscious of perfect peace, happiness, joy, interest, abundance and so on. "I am conscious of perfect harmony, happiness and joy. All is perfect." If you do this you will find yourself moving to a better position, either in the same firm, or with another one; and you will not obtain your promotion at anyone else's expense.

Once you know how to treat there is no more competition for you. Treatment is creative and will produce customers and opportunities, without taking from anyone else.

No matter what the dilemma is, treat and the best for all concerned must happen.

When you have no earthly resources of any kind is just the time when treatment is most powerful. Man's extremity is God's opportunity.

A GENERAL DAILY TREATMENT

An excellent method of Daily Treatment for beginners is to read a chapter of the Bible, or a few pages of Emerson, or any book that you find helpful.

Then say, "I am not my body. I am not my thoughts. I am not my feelings. I am not my psyche. These are only my servants. I am Pneuma. I am Divine Spirit. I have dominion. All my conditions are spiritual." Take up anything that may be troubling you at the moment and claim freedom.

Work against prejudice, which keeps many out of the kingdom when they least suspect it.

Claim Spiritual Perception and Spiritual Understanding.

If you are irritable treat yourself everyday for sheer Good Humor. This alone will solve a surprising number of your problems and is tremendously effective in self-healing.

You can measure your progress by the rate at which you are getting rid of condemnation and resentment.

Emmet Fox

Part Two

THE SCIENCE OF LIVING

As I think you know, this teaching deals with the whole of life, with existence as it is, and it is something much more than psychology.

In order to get a right view about life, the first thing is to realize what you are yourself. You must know what you are, and not merely what you think you are. You must know what God is, and you must know what the universe around you is—these are the three things.

In order to understand yourself you have to understand what God is. Nobody supposes for a moment that finite people can get a full comprehension of God, but we can get quite a good working knowledge of God, and you cannot know the truth about yourself unless you have the right idea about God. And you cannot have a correct idea about God and yourself unless you know what the world about you is. These are three in one, and one in three. You continually find the idea of the Trinity coming up.

There are different ways of regarding man according to what your object is, but for our purpose the best way is to follow St. Paul's classification and divide him into three parts, namely, body, soul, and spirit.

These are not three men—there is only one man, but at first we seem to have three things.

This body that you see is physical, and you know perfectly well that it is not the real you. Probably no one on earth who looks into the mirror would say, "That is the real me."

The second part is the soul ("soul" with a small "s") better called, as in the Greek Testament, the *psyche*. This, the human mind, is what constitutes your personality.

The third part St. Paul calls *Pneuma*, the spirit. That is the Greek word from which our familiar word pneumatic comes.

Conventional religion speaks, as a rule, of the body and soul only, but this is a deadly error, and that is why the orthodox teaching has done so little in the many centuries during which it held full sway. We do not condemn orthodoxy, for Truth comes not to condemn but to fulfill. If you find it helpful to keep up attendance at church, etc., by all means do so. This teaching will enrich your life; it will not take anything away. If you find the old things drop away, as probably you will, well and good. Do not feel that you have lost anything. Do not feel that you have left that God to come over to this God, as it were. There is and always has been only one God, of course, and now you are enlarging your former ideas, that is all.

Pneuma is your real self; the real you. Each of us has this real self behind the psyche. It is the divine part of us. Call it your higher self, or your real self, or the Divine Spark, what you please, it is there, and it never gets ill, or tired, or angry. It was never born, it has existed from all eternity, and it will never die. It has never made any mistakes and knows neither fear nor anxiety. It is always in full communion with God. It is what makes us men and women and not animals. It is what people really refer to when they speak of the Inner Light. We are not evolved animals, and God is always present within us to heal and teach us.

The science that deals with the physical body is called physiology. It is a description, quite correct as far as it goes, of how the physical body is seen to work. That the blood circulates, and so on.

Psychology is the next step behind this; it describes how the psyche works, and is also very useful, as far as it goes. It will help us to make the most of our human mind, such as it is. At the same time our own efforts are such feeble things at best that really even in the most favorable cases there is not much to be done. What is called Practical Psychology is usually a training in personal efficiency, business methods, and autosuggestion.

But this teaching deals essentially with Pneuma, or the real spiritual man, and it is only when you come to Pneuma that you touch the miracle. Then it is not a question of improving things, but of realizing existing perfection. It does not urge you to go in for exercise or relaxing, or open windows though these are all excellent things, to be heartily recommended. This teaching is concerned exclusively with spiritual things.

This is the teaching given by Jesus as recorded

in the Four Gospels. It is true Christianity. When you have got a grip of this teaching and have accomplished some healings, then go back and reread the Gospels again in the light of your new knowledge, and you will be astonished that you so long missed the essential points.

Jesus deals entirely with states of consciousness. He never tells you to do this or that. The Mohammedans are forbidden to eat pork, as are the Jews, and the Hindus must not eat the flesh of the ox or the cow, and so on; but Jesus deals only with states of consciousness, because he knew that if your consciousness is in the right condition you must find yourself eating the right food, saying and doing the right things, and demonstrating harmony in every way, while, if the consciousness is wrong, nothing else can be really right.

We are concerned exclusively with states of consciousness, not with outside things, but, nevertheless, we have to understand how we are made up, in order to do our work.

The physical body is composed of what we call "matter," that is, solids, liquids, and gases, but there is a fourth state of matter called ether, a much finer and usually impalpable form, and the psyche is made of ether. So the psyche is material but not physical; it is etheric.

Ether exists in various densities, and your human mind, or soul, or psyche is etheric, and it is the repository of all your thoughts, in fact it is really one mass of thoughts. What we call thought, human thought, is the activity of this ether, something like the wireless signals but much finer. It is the state of the psyche at any moment that makes you what you are.

What we were in the habit of calling our mind (psyche) turns out to be only a very small proportion of what we really have. By far the greater proportion is subconscious, or unconscious, or not consciously known to ourselves. We do not know what is going on there, but all sorts of interesting and important things are going on. It expresses the truth well to say that about 97 percent of the psyche is subconscious, and only about 3 percent conscious.

It is the subconscious that directly governs your life, for humanly speaking you are what your subconscious mind thinks you are.

The conscious mind and the subconscious have each their own characteristics and their own functions, and the first difference is this, that the conscious mind has the faculty of inductive logic or common sense.

Again, the conscious mind has little strength and a limited field of attention.

The subconscious, on the other hand, seems to have unlimited strength. One reason why we find it so difficult sometimes to manage ourselves, to break bad habits, such as smoking or lying too long in bed, is owing to this tremendous strength of the subconscious. Not understanding how to work, people push in one direction with the feeble strength of the conscious, while the immense power of the subconscious is pushing the opposite direction, and so they fail.

The subconscious has a perfect memory. You can regard it as a perfect card index. It has a record of every thought you have ever held in your life, many of which you were never conscious, all the things you have ever seen or heard, all the people you have met and every book you have read. In fact, it is a complete record of your life. Compare it to a Gramophone record. It is not obvious, it makes no noise, but the tune is there and can be obtained by the proper

79

means at any time. This is the "Judgment Books" spoken of in Scripture. This is why it is important to be very careful what we allow to enter our minds, not to revel in accounts of crimes, or diseases, and in general, to be particular about the sort of company, human or literary, that we keep. It all goes down and will be demonstrated sooner or later, unless wiped out by treatment. But it is much less trouble to keep error out of the mind than to get rid of it when once it has got in.

We live in a universe that is governed by law. There are laws of physics, laws of mechanics, etc., but *treatment*, which is the action of God, will override any of these laws. Apart from treatment, however, you are under the law, and as long as you are under the law you have to take what is coming to you; you have to take the result of your deeds and your thoughts. When you turn to God for help you come under Grace, and that will set you free from any natural laws for a good purpose. You can overtake your mistakes and wipe out the consequences. Otherwise the Law is ruthless.

As we look round the world we seem to be separate people, quite cut off one from another, but this is not really so. All subconscious minds are joined together underneath, and so, the human race is really one. You might say that we are all limbs of the one body. This is why telepathy is possible. That is why Absent Treatments are possible. That is why selfishness is always such bad policy, for when we injure someone else we really injure ourselves. This fact has been more or less dimly known to philosophers in all ages. The age-old comparison of the Archipelago is still excellent. We are just like a group of islands. They seem all to be separate portions of land, but we know that they are not, because they are all joined up under the sea, so that you could sink a shaft in one island, dig a tunnel, and come up in another one.

The portion of the island above the water represents the conscious, the submerged portion the subconscious, and the main portion of the earth stands for the Race Mind.

You have certain defects and difficulties that are peculiar to yourself, and these are located in your own subconscious, but also you have many limitations not peculiar to yourself but common to the whole human race, and these come to you from the Race Mind. Such beliefs as, that you cannot live under water, that you need sleep, or that certain substances called "poisons" are deadly.

The term "Superconscious" is often used nowadays. It is another name for God. It is used to indicate the vital fact that God is only to be found within ourselves. People are always trying to find God somewhere outside of themselves, and that is why they so often fail to find Him. He is only to be found within.

Remember that you must be the master of the subconscious, but when it comes to the Superconscious then you have to be the pupil.

You will never be able to arrange your life satisfactorily until you become the master of your subconscious, and this brings us to the power of thought. In this material world in which we are living nothing matters except thought. The whole universe is just one huge network of thoughts. Bodies, houses, trees, rocks, animals, stars and planets, all are but externalized thoughts.

The principal thing with which we shall concern ourselves is the healing of the body and affairs, so let us begin with the body. What, then, is the physical body? The answer to this will be the critical point in healing.

The answer is that the body is but an aggregate of thoughts, the outpicturing of your psyche. Nothing can appear in the body that is not first in the soul. A cut finger is but the outpicturing of the thought of a cut finger, a boil is but the outpicturing of the thought of a boil, and so on. There is no difference, really, between the wound, and this thought of the wound. If the error thought can be got out of the mind it must disappear from the body, and spiritual healing consists in getting the thought out of the mind. In spiritual healing you never do anything to the body, you treat the psyche. If you remove the trouble by physical means you do something to the body but leave the psyche untouched, this may be a cure but it is not a healing. Healing means *making whole*.

So the body is not a kind of garment or case on the soul; it is the outpicturing of the soul.

TREATMENT

The word *treatment* is a new one to many people. It means Scientific Prayer, as distinguished from ordinary prayer. What is prayer?

Emmet Fox

Prayer is thinking about God. If you are thinking about God you are praying, and all written prayers and liturgies, all hymns, all church rituals, are simply so many means to help you to think about God. The word *prayer* is usually kept for the old-fashioned type of prayer, that is, supplicatory prayer, in which God is asked to do something. People say, "Please, God, cure my headache," or "Please, God, get me out of this difficulty," and often they hardly expect the prayer to be answered. Yet Jesus has told us that prayer is a science, and if it is a science, then, clearly, there should be no room for uncertainty. He said, "Ye shall ask what ye will, and it shall be done unto you." (John 15:7). The ordinary way of praying is not very helpful. We have all prayed for certain things, and have not received any answer. When we pray scientifically, however, that is when we use treatment, all our prayers are answered sooner or later, if we are working rightly. If the thing we want is good for us, we get it. If it is not good for us, the result of the treatment is that we come to see that this is so, and we cease to want it. Then as a rule we get something else instead, but in all cases we get satisfaction.

Scientific prayer, or treatment, concerns Pneuma. Instead of asking God to put something right in the material world we turn right away from the appearance of evil or lack, and dwell upon the already existing perfection in the real world. We *realize* or make real to ourselves the unchangeable fact that the True Man, Pneuma, is absolutely perfect now in every respect, expressing God in perfect harmony. If one can get a sufficiently clear realization of this, the trouble, whatever it is, will disappear, and we shall find ourselves in peace and safety. One must not, however, speculate as to how the solution will come. This is called *outlining*.

OUTLINING

Outlining means thinking of a particular way out of your difficulty. This is wrong because you must leave the mode of action to God. All that concerns you is to get out of the trouble, whatever it is. Leave the solution to Infinite Wisdom, and it will usually turn out to be something infinitely better than anything you could have imagined yourself. As a matter of fact any tendency to outline usually has the effect of delaying the demonstration, besides being wrong in itself.

If a headache is troubling you, instead of saying, "Here's this headache again," say, "I am the child of God. My real self is Divine Spirit. It has no pain; it has perfect peace, health and happiness." Say this quietly but earnestly, and endeavor to feel what you are saying, and if you get even a small degree of realization, the headache will presently disappear.

Note that you do not say that the material you has not a headache. This would be a lie. You affirm the perfect harmony of your real spiritual self, Pneuma. The statement, then, is eternal Truth, and it is Truth that heals.

If you were on a sinking ship, and you stopped thinking of the material surroundings, shipwreck, ocean, etc., and dwelt, instead, on the Truth, namely that your real self, Pneuma, lives, forever, in the presence of God, in perfect peace and safety, you would be saved.

Of course, in such a case it would be very difficult at first to get away from the material picture, but by steadily carrying on treatment you would presently succeed. It has been done many times.

Jesus said that when we pray we are to believe that we have received (Matthew 21:22, Mark 11:24). Now this could not refer to your material self; to think that you have something when you have not is to think a lie; and so it must refer to the real man, Pneuma, concerning whom it would be quite true.

So we see that the secret of scientific prayer is to stop thinking of the world of appearances, and to think of God instead. The word *God* in its fullest sense includes the Spiritual Man and Heaven, for as they are the expression of God, they are the Presence of God as manifestation.

Stop brooding over your troubles and think of your true self instead; then the troubles will disappear. Lifelong habit may cause you to feel a strong desire to think over these unpleasant things, and even to rehearse them at length, but this must be overcome.

If you have done something wrong, proceed in just the same way. Stop thinking of the error or sin, and realize that your true self is the expression of God and has never sinned. This will free you from the sin, i.e., you will not repeat it, and it will also save you and others from any consequences thereof. Note particularly that this does not mean that one may sin with impunity and then escape the penalty by treatment. This would be absurd. As long as we sin we shall bring punishment upon ourselves, and there is no escape. But when once the sin is abandoned, there is no longer any good purpose to be served by punishment, and as nature is never vindictive, it ceases. Many people have longed earnestly to abandon some sin that held them in bondage, such as drunkenness, and have miserably failed to do so while relying on their own efforts. Treatment, however, if steadily applied, never fails in such cases. When the work is properly done the sin itself goes first, then the desire to sin in that way, and finally, the sinner or patient being now completely reformed, all unhappy consequences of his former sin can be made to disappear too. This is *the forgiveness of sins*, and one sees that it is the perfect union of Justice and Mercy.

HEALING

Healing of others is carried out in just the same way as the healing of oneself. When someone comes to you in trouble or in pain, listen to what they have to say, but hold the thought all the time, "His real self (Pneuma) has no pain, or trouble. He is divine and spiritual." The first few times you will have to say, "His real self has not got this trouble" or "My real self has not got it," but presently it will be possible for you to say, "He has not got it," or "I have not got it." You will thoroughly understand that you are talking about Pneuma.

The essential course of a treatment is like this. A person comes to you and says, "I am very ill. I am in great pain." You will silently affirm, "No, he is not in pain, he is divine spirit. He is free and well." You know that this is true, but at first you do not feel it. The thought of the sick man is much more vivid than the thought of the spiritual one. You accept the truth but you do not realize it. Then you go on making statements of Truth about the patient, which is the "treatment." Presently you do begin to realize spiritual perfection a little, and then gradually more and more.

As the treatment goes on the sense of the sick man gets less and less, and the realization of the Divine Being becomes stronger and stronger. When the sense of the perfect spiritual being is stronger than the sense of the sick man, the patient will be healed.

We do not deny that the illness is there as a passing belief, but only that it is not a reality. We deal with Pneuma.

Some people use many words in a treatment, others few. Some have a few affirmations only, which they use over and over again. Some people speak quickly, some very slowly. Just find your own way.

The two weapons that you have to use are the *denial* and the *affirmation*. They constitute the two-edged sword of Scripture.

Anything that you affirm will come into your life, to the extent that you believe the affirmation.

In the same way you can deny evil out of your life into its native nothingness.

If you say often, "I am a miserable sinner," and believe it, that is the quickest way to become one. In like manner if you say, "I am the image and likeness of God," that will also begin to be seen as true.

The denial is to say, "I am not afraid" or "There is no pain." It refers, of course, to Pneuma.

What is your spiritual self like? It has no shape, for it is a thing outside of space. It is an individualized consciousness. It has certain capacities, powers, and capabilities, which we see as the various parts of the body. For example, it can think, that capacity we see in a limited way as the head.

It reflects, or expresses God as Life, and that we see as the heart.

It expresses God as Love, and that we see as the blood.

It has understanding, and that we know as hearing.

It is perfectly truthful and understands truth, and that we see as the kidneys.

Our eyes represent spiritual perception.

The hand is the power of manifestation.

It is very helpful to work under one or more of the Main Aspects of God, thus for blood poisoning, realize God as Love; for kidney trouble, God as Truth.

For nerve troubles take God under all aspects, but especially as Intelligence.

You can always treat in general terms, but as a rule it is quicker to work under one of these points.

Give yourself at least a quarter of an hour's treatment every day; much longer if possible, but not less. Never force it. Never make a burden of it.

You can think independently of space and time. You can think of China as easily and as quickly as you can think of the other side this room. You can think of next year before it comes, so our minds are free of space and time.

There are two types of treatment, the Man and the Woman. The Man is the active treatment; most treatments are of this type. The Woman type is rather passive—you just pause and feel the Presence of God. This is usually the best and always the quickest, but you cannot always get it. Treatment is always businesslike and definite. It is never sentimental or vague.

A FORM OF TREATMENT

1. Think of God or heaven.
2. Deny the existence of the trouble in heaven.
3. Affirm harmony for the Spiritual Man and keep doing so until you feel satisfied.

Pity, in the ordinary sense, is a false luxury and must be driven out of the mind. It injures both you and the victim. Do not pity him. Treat, and help him instead.

Nothing but good can come out of treatment, good for everybody. You will never get anything from treatment at anybody else's expense. The best will happen for everybody.

The real motive for treating is to be loyal to God.

BODY

Your body and your affairs at any moment are but the out picturing of your soul, so if you want to know what the state of your soul is, well, just look about you at your body and affairs and you will see.

It is true that people often have ugly bodies and beautiful souls, just as a cripple may have a beautiful character, but the explanation is this. The cripple may be wonderfully advanced on other points, but his subconscious thought is wrong about body. On the other hand an athlete of perfect physique may be a person of defective character. This means that the individual's idea of body is excellent although his soul is wrong in other respects. In this world there is strict justice in the sense that you get exactly according to your thought in all cases. This man's conception of body is good and so we find him with a good body, which is only fair. Again a case has been cited of a man whose business was a great success, and yet his private life was very bad. Here again he will surely bring punishment upon himself for the evil that he is responsible for, but in the meantime his thought is right about business, and so he gets the benefit of that.

There are different departments of life, and you get according to your thought. If business is going wrong you are thinking wrongly about business. Think rightly and it will come right. If you have bad health you are thinking wrongly about body. When there is a bad or weak side to the life it means that there has been wrong thinking.

Now we come to consider the truth about God. The only thing really worth doing is to get a better knowledge of God, for everything else follows from that. You may say, "No, because one has to get a living, eat and drink, and so on," but this is a mistake since, in fact, all these things will follow automatically from a correct knowledge of God. ("Seek ye first the Kingdom of God and all these things will be added.") If our idea of God is adequate everything will go well with us, and on the contrary, if it is very inferior, everything will go amiss. If we think that God does not provide for His children we shall find ourselves in poverty before long.

Actually there is no joy or happiness apart from God, as you will see when you understand what God is. People often seek satisfaction in what is wrong, as for example in drink, but this is a radical mistake, which always defeats itself. On the other hand we need not be always saying our prayers in set form, for whenever we are enjoying ourselves in a legitimate way that joy is the expression of God.

Most people have a totally inadequate conception of God, because we all get our first notion of Him when we are very young, and seldom is it afterwards revised. As children we think of God probably as just a big man. Then, as we grow up, we alter all our other ideas in accordance with our growing capacities, except, too often just this, the most important one of all. In many cases this is never reconsidered.

Emmet Fox

In order to get a more adequate concept of God you have to begin by asking yourself the question: What is God really like? Could you meet Him, for instance? I used to have a vague idea that I should meet God by going up to a desk. This, of course, is impossible, for it would mean that God has a limited form.

We cannot grasp the full truth about God because we are finite, but we can get a splendid idea of God for practical purposes if we work in the right way.

There are twelve Main Aspects of God, of which only seven are known to humanity in the present stage, and the best way to build up your knowledge of God is to think over these seven aspects frequently, affirming that you express them and understand them; that is to say, that Pneuma, your real self, does.

The Seven Aspects are:

LIFE, TRUTH, LOVE, INTELLIGENCE, SOUL, SPIRIT, PRINCIPLE.

The first three are the most important and really include every quality of God, the rest being somewhat secondary. When you are giving a treatment you usually work on one or more of these aspects. Other of the attributes of God

96

are omnipotence, omniscience, omnipresence, beauty, joy, wisdom, and so on. They are not main aspects, but they follow from them.

These seven aspects do not mean that God exists, as it were, in seven different ways. It does not mean that there are seven persons in God. God is one, and He knows Himself in infinite ways, but with our limited seeing we have to get our knowledge of Him in these seven aspects. Of course you could not really have one aspect without the others. You cannot have Truth without Love, or either without Life. Compare a rose. That has different qualities and we have to consider them separately, color, smell, shape, weight, but the rose actually has them all, all the time. You could not get color without weight or shape, etc. God is everywhere fully present in every one of His qualities.

PNEUMA

Now we come to consider Pneuma, the Spiritual Man, your real self. This is the real you, your true identity. It is spiritual, and so now you will see that it must be substance, and so it will have all the qualities, which we have just seen, belong to substance.

Emmet Fox

Your health, and the harmony of your whole life, will depend entirely on the extent to which you identify yourself in thought with your real self, Pneuma. The Bible tells us that God has made man in His own image and likeness, and that is true, but of course it refers to Pneuma. The limited man that we know could not possibly be the image and likeness of God. Pneuma is the child of God and the offspring is always of the same species as the parent. No one ever heard of a rose growing on a lily plant, or a cow giving birth to a pony. The law is that each seed brings forth after its own kind. The spiritual man is one with God, but he is not one and the same. That is why he is called an individual. Individual means undivided. It is not possible to grasp with the human intellect how two can be one, and yet not one and the same; but by treatment you will be able to realize it within your own consciousness. In the material world when a man makes a table he sends it away to the market and is done with it. In like manner we and our children are not one. We may die but they live on, or they may die and we live on. We are separate beings. But God and the spiritual man are one, though not one and the same.

They may be compared to the singer and her song. The song is not the singer, but neither is it something separate and distinct from her. It really expresses every part of her nature, for the singer's instrument is her whole body. If she died the song would stop; if she were ill or angry the song would give evidence of the fact, and so on. Anyone sufficiently sensitive could read her whole character and history in that song. And so man expresses every quality of God. Pneuma is at one with God, and lives always in full communion with God; that is to say in heaven.

HEAVEN

Heaven is the popular name for the world of reality. Where is heaven? Heaven is just here, round about us now where we are. Why do we not experience it then? Why do we find all sorts of inharmony and sickness instead? The answer is that by the abuse of our free-will we have tuned ourselves out from heaven, much as a radio set can be tuned out from a particular station into another wave length, and that we always get the kind of surroundings and experience for which we are attuned. All improvement really consists in tuning back into heaven, and this tuning back is called prayer or treatment. This process is the real atonement, which can better be taken in the sense of at-one-ment. If you are in any sort of difficulty and you can only realize strongly enough that your real self dwells in the presence of God, you will find that the difficulty will disappear. If a convict were to realize this fact sufficiently he would find himself discharged from prison, a free and a reformed man.

What is heaven like? *Heaven is the Presence of God.* It is a world of perfect ideas, all expressing God. Man does not see God face to face in heaven because that would mean that God was finite, but he feels the presence of God. The *face* means the power of recognition. A world of "ideas" may seem at first sight rather thin and unsubstantial, but the exact opposite is the case. A spiritual idea is the real substance of things; our so-called material objects are the shadows by comparison. The number of ideas in heaven are infinite, and the spiritual man always has an unlimited abundance of them. Spiritual ideas lie behind all the objects that you see about you. What is the spiritual idea laying behind a chair? Do not think of a kind of ghostly chair: the true idea is man's ability to rest. The true idea behind a jug would be the ability to hold certain ideas or combinations of ideas together. In other words the world that you see about you is your limited, false seeing of the real spiritual world.

The treatment for a material object that is giving trouble, such as a machine out of order, or something broken or missing, is to realize the spiritual nature (not necessarily the exact spiritual reality, which in many cases is not known) of the object in question. The result will then depend entirely on the degree of realization that you get. Either the trouble will come right, or you will get a new article, or the old one will be satisfactorily repaired; but you will overcome your difficulty in some way. Never imagine that it is wrong to treat about seeming trifles. There are no trifles. Everything, great or small, must be right. Your duty is to demonstrate peace of mind, harmony, serenity at all points. Neither must you allow yourself to regard such homely things as boots, shirts, chairs and tables as beneath praying for. We must have these things in abundance in order not to have to worry about them.

Whenever you want something it is a sign that your real self has already got the idea corresponding to that thing. Realize this fact and it will come into your possession, if it is good for you. Often we think that we want something although really we do not, and if we got it we should soon be tired of it, and again we often think we want something that would be positively injurious for us, as with the drunkard's desire for drink. In such cases as these the result of the treatment would be that the false desire would fall away. It is always safe to treat, for nothing but good can come of it.

So we see that God is everywhere present, that He is Life, Truth, and Love, knows everything and can do anything and only sends harmony, peace, and joy; that He never produces or endorses pain, sickness or suffering. He never punishes anyone. God is the father, and man is the child, and God expresses Himself by means of man. There are an infinite number of spiritual beings in heaven, every one different and every one perfect, and we see about two thousand millions of them in a limited way as the inhabitants of this globe. Each man is an individual enterprise on the part of God, so no two of them are alike.

DEMONSTRATION

The answer to a treatment is called a *demonstration*, because it demonstrates the harmony of life. To demonstrate, according to Webster, means to so clearly show a thing to be true that the opposite will be seen to be ridiculous.

If you give very little time to spiritual things your treatments will not have a very large content.

Treatment is not contemplation or meditation; it is actively thinking about God.

An excellent thing to do is to take a piece of paper and write down as many things as you can think of about God. "God is everywhere. God is wisdom. God is beauty," and so on.

You must be continually making experiments in treatment. Try treating for all sorts of things. That is the way to learn. One advantage in treating for little things is that the result is usually known almost at once, and therefore you will be able to tell whether you are working rightly.

The first time that you see the success of one of your own treatments, and get the thrill of conscious power within you, you meet the Rider on the White Horse.

TREATING FOR INSPIRATION

All students of this teaching try at least to treat about their difficulties, but many seem never to work for inspiration. The two wings of the movement are (or should be) Healing and Inspiration. The direct inspiration of God can always be got in some degree by treatment.

In order to succeed in business or in any profession it is necessary to evince a certain amount of originality. True originality is only to be got by treatment. If you require any piece of information for a good purpose you can get it by treatment. It might be some kind of statistics or some fact about nature for research purposes; you could get it and save much time. You can be continually guided in your affairs. This is the true way to "take God for your partner."

The way to treat for inspiration, as with all other good, is to claim it persistently. You claim it by affirming that your real self, Pneuma, already has it now. Say, "God is guiding me" or "The Christ is guiding me. I have all the knowledge I need. I understand this. I know what to do."

The Science of Living

By this time you should be able to give up talking about your "real" self. It should be a matter of course that when you treat you are thinking of Pneuma. Henceforth let the word "I" in treatment always mean Pneuma. Your object will be to forget all about the material man for the time being.

If you really want the inspiration of God you must put your own opinions aside, but this is just the last thing that people will do. They feel sure they know just what to do, and only consult God in a halfhearted way. Often the inspired guidance is in direct conflict with our own views. If your business is not a success it is a sign that your ideas on the subject are incorrect, and therefore it is only to be expected that the way of wisdom in that matter will be at variance with your own ideas. Otherwise you would have made a success of it. And so if you want the truth about anything you must be prepared to give up all prejudices and habitual views. God will not force Himself upon you. You will have to wait for harmony until you are tired of muddle and failure and will look to God.

Be definite in treatment. If you want a house treat for a house, and not just for harmony and peace, etc., but do not outline either, that is to say, do not fix your attention on any particular house. If you do, the chances are that it will not turn out well. Realize right place; man is always conscious of the right ideas.

While it is wrong to outline, yet you should always expect satisfaction. The outlining would consist in making up your mind precisely how that satisfaction would come about.

No treatment is ever wasted. Every time that you think of God in the full sense of the word ("God" includes man and heaven for they are His manifestation), you improve your life in every respect.

In certain cases when the demonstration is made you get a beautiful clear feeling, and you know that the work is done. This is not always so, however, and you must not think that the case will not be cleared merely because you do not get that sense.

Occasionally when you are working for some difficulty, usually for yourself, the very presence of God breaks in upon you. It is a foretaste of heaven. There is nothing else in life like it. This is referred to in the Bible as the alighting of a dove. "He saw the heavens opened and the Holy

The Science of Living

Spirit in the likeness of a dove descending upon him." When this happens, when the dove alights, do not do any more treatment for that particular thing. Leave it absolutely alone.

Otherwise you cannot treat too much for anything, provided that it is real treatment. It is, however, possible to go on treating when you are in a state of mind that has been described as waterlogged. This is bad. If you feel like this, drop it and change the subject. Go to the theatre, or talk to a friend until you get away from it for a time. Then with a fresh mind go at it again.

If you ever feel that you cannot treat when you want to, do not on any account try to force it by will power. Be quiet and simply hold the thought of one of the Main Aspects without attempting to think. Presently you will find yourself treating easily.

Always avoid tenseness in all your mental working. This is fatal. Be natural. Be easy. Be informal and spontaneous. Seriousness is not earnestness. Undue gravity may be only a cloak for stupidity or pride.

Of course you cannot have too much reverence for God, but do not let reverence grow into fear. We should turn to God as easily as a child turns to its father. It is no compliment to the parent if the child is afraid of him.

Do not allow yourself to have any fads about treatment. Some people cannot treat (as they think) with their eyes open. This is wrong. Train yourself to treat in any circumstances. Start off without any ceremony. Have no preliminaries.

The Christ healing is the quick "woman" way of healing. It is the best way, but you cannot always or often get it.

The Healing Christ is the realization of the presence of God within you—Christ in you, the hope of glory. Christ in *you*, not in someone else.

You do not seek a knowledge of God in order to do something with that knowledge. That knowledge in itself is what brings the healing. No invalid can have a good, all-round understanding of God, or he would not be an invalid.

Treat for a car because that will help to make your life complete.

Treat a headache because that is making your life incomplete.

While you are treating keep the thought, "God is making this treatment."

No matter how many times you have treated before for the same thing make each treatment a fresh work. Never copy the last treatment. Begin each time where you left off before. This keeps the thing alive.

Have no rules for treatment; rules shut out the Holy Ghost.

The art of treatment is this; to get away in thought from the material condition. In the East they call this "disjunction." Get immersed in God. Someone once said, "Go straight to heaven, and do not take your trouble with you." A lady said, "When things are going wrong I get well into God."

Be insistent, but not vehement, which is tiring. You must not accept less than harmony. You must not take "no" for an answer. Jesus taught this in two parables, the importunate widow, and the householder who was disturbed in the night.

A FORM OF TREATMENT

Get by yourself and either pray or treat or read the Bible or some devotional book until you feel the presence of God, a little bit at least.

Then ask Him for what you want; and then return thanks there and then for the demonstration. (See John 11:41-42.)

This form of treatment will not be much use unless you succeed in getting some actual feeling of the Presence. If you cannot succeed in this, or if you cannot return thanks beforehand with conviction, you will have to rely on one of the other forms. Otherwise this form is very effective. You must state what you want with decision and exactness. A suitable house. The rent that is due on Saturday. Peace with your friend (with whom, let us say, you have quarreled) and so on.

When you are treating about something, or having treatment from another, never discuss the subject with other people or allow them to know that the work is being done. When the demonstration is made keep it to yourself for some time, unless there is an obvious reason for telling it. After a time tell it, to glorify God and help your fellow man.

Keep a register of all your good demonstrations from the very beginning, with notes of any special circumstances.

THE SPIRITUAL BASIS

The time has now arrived when you can get a clear understanding of what life really is. To get that understanding is to be on the Spiritual Basis. This is by far the most important thing in your whole existence. It is a perfectly definite position. You are either on the Spiritual Basis, or you are not; there is no middle way.

We have seen that God cannot possibly be just a big man or woman; it matters not how big or strong, or wise. Our natural tendency is to think of Him in this way in the beginning. It has been said that if an insect could think as we do, and could think about God, it would imagine that God was a huge insect of unlimited powers. We, too, make God after our own image and likeness, and this breaks the first commandment, for it is idolatry. We know, also, that our real self is not this limited faulty human being with which we are so familiar, but a divine spiritual being, the image and likeness of God Himself.

Just as we see ourselves in this limited and defective way, so, we see heaven in which we really are now, all wrong. Most of it we do not

111

see at all, and what we do see is minimized and distorted by the human mind until it is very much like looking out on the street through that fluted glass that causes one to see everything bent and twisted out of shape. The people and things in the street are quite normal, really, but our vision of them is awry, and it needs only to get rid of the misleading windowpane by opening the window in order to see their true nature. So it is with Reality, and that is why Jesus said, "Know the Truth, and the Truth will set you free."

We can also compare the same thing to the experience of a color-blind man. He sees the same world that we do, but he sees it all wrong. All blacks, whites and grays. What does a beautiful flower garden convey to him? Nothing like what it means to a person with normal color sight. And so we see the world of reality, or heaven, all wrong. The difference between, say, a broken tea cup and a whole one is that in the former case you see the spiritual idea in a more limited way. If you want a cup and have not got one it means that the spiritual idea is there, but you cannot perceive it. The important thing is to understand that there are not two worlds.

The Science of Living

There is only one world, God's world seen by us at present in the wrong way.

You have seen that humanly speaking you are a soul or psyche, and that you have a body. Many people seem to think that man is a body, and has a soul, but this is a fundamental mistake. The reverse is the truth, and now we have to ask ourselves, since, as we have seen, the body and circumstances are but the outpicturing of the psyche at any moment, why certain thoughts are visibly expressed and others are not. At any given moment you have all sorts of thoughts and opinions in your mind. Thoughts of illness, hopes of healing, doubts, fears, speculations, prejudices and the whole welter of beliefs and half-beliefs that make up the mentality of the average man or woman. Now some of these thoughts are demonstrated externally and others are not, and why is this? The answer, quite simply, is this. You demonstrate only those thoughts that you really believe in. Those you *really* believe in. Mere pious opinions or vague peradventures are not demonstrated, but only our true convictions; well, look about you. If you want to know your real conviction of body, look in the glass. Your real conviction about supply? Consult your bank book. Your real conviction about your fellow man? Look at the people with whom you live and work. Your real conviction about God's providence? Look at your home and general surroundings. These things, the external circumstances of your life, are the perfect register of your actual convictions at any moment. There is no getting away from this. This is the fact, and neither fear nor favor can alter it. So true is it that deceit and hypocrisy are mere waste of time, for you cannot deceive your own soul, and it is your own soul, and nothing and no one else on earth, that controls every second of your life.

Remember it is your conviction that matters, and so healing really consists in bringing about a different conviction in the soul of your patient.

If you say, "I think the Cunard is a fine line of steamers, but I absolutely refuse to travel by it; I must go by the White Star or nothing," that shows your real conviction about the Cunard. Whatever is wrong in your life represents your real conviction at that point. A cut, or a diseased lung, is your real conviction. You may hold in theory that you are divine spirit, but your real conviction is on the side of the ailment. Change the conviction; make your belief in yourself as spirit the conviction, and the body will be healed.

This means that no matter what your difficulty may be you have nothing to deal with but your own thoughts, for nothing else can come into your experience.

You will easily see that this is the most tremendous fact in the whole range of life. No other piece of knowledge can come within a million miles of it in importance. No other information matters really when once you know that. This is the keystone of the teaching. This is the critical point at which it differs from all other religions.

When once you have grasped this point you cease wasting time on the thousand and one things that used to divert your attention from the only thing that matters. For instance you stop blaming other people once and for all. Usually the first thing that the human mind does when it finds itself in any trouble is to look round for someone else to lay the blame on. Now we see that such a procedure is only childish, and we get on with the business instead, and destroy the false conviction, which is our real enemy. Then we are free.

Further, you will now see that it means that it makes no matter what trouble there may be in your life, there is a way out, since you have nothing to deal with but your own thoughts; and as we all know, we have power to select and control our thoughts, difficult though it may be at times to do so. As long as you thought that your destiny was in the hands of other people the situation was hopeless. People say, "It is useless for me to struggle because of such and such a reason. If only I had a profession. If only I had married someone else. If only I had not bought this business. If I had gone abroad when I had the chance," and so on. But now you know that this is a mistake, because you have nothing to deal with but your own thoughts.

Remind yourself of this fact constantly. Repeat it to yourself a hundred times a day until you really do begin to grasp all that it means to you. Write it down where you will see it often. Have it on your desk, or wherever you work. Hang it in your bedroom where you will easily see it. Write it in your pocket book. Write it on your soul, by constantly dwelling upon it. It will transform your life. It will lead you out of the land of Egypt and out of the House of Bondage.

If your trouble is indigestion, get that thought out of your mind, and you will be healed. If it is poverty, get rid of that belief, and money will fall out of the sky if necessary. Suppose you are being threatened with a lawsuit; well, you have nothing to deal with but your own thoughts, so get them right, and the lawsuit will collapse. Realize love and harmony and the Allness of the One Mind. You cannot get rid of fear or anger by will power. It is useless to say, "I will not be angry," for if the provocation is sufficient it will overcome your resolution. It can only be done by treatment. If the house is on fire, get that thought out of your mind and you will be safe, and your property too. And so on right throughout life.

I think we have now reached the stage when we can answer the fundamental question, what actually is this material world in which we seem to live and work and suffer? What does the metaphysician mean when he says that there is no matter? What does the mystic mean when he says that all is illusion? These statements appear either inexplicable or absurd to the casual hearer, and often they irritate him very much, especially if he is in difficulties at the time he hears them. The explanation is this. What we call the material world is actually a state of consciousness. It is not a separate external thing or agglomeration of things. It is simply the state of consciousness, which we are holding at the moment.

"Well and good," says someone, "but what then, is a state of consciousness?" The best way to understand what a state of consciousness is, is to consider several alternative states of consciousness with which we are all familiar. This so-called "normal" state is not the only one of which we have knowledge. First of all there is the ordinary dream. We are all so accustomed to dreaming that we seldom give the experience a second thought, but if you had dreamt last night for the first time, you would be able to talk of nothing else all day.

The important thing to note about a dream is that while it lasts it seems to be absolutely real and true. To the dreamer it is true. A person, let us say, is asleep in bed in Kensington, but she is dreaming that she is in Switzerland

The Science of Living

where she spent her holidays last year. There she is, as she thinks, surrounded by the snow-clad peaks. You, however, who are what we call "awake," go into the room and say she is lying in bed in London. Now suppose that her sister is also asleep, within perhaps a few inches of her, but is dreaming that she is on a ship crossing the Atlantic. Around her are miles and miles of ocean. Here we have three different states of consciousness, the Switzerland of one sleeper, the Atlantic of the other, and the London of the spectator, and in one sense they may all be said to coexist and to interpenetrate one another.

Another well-known state of consciousness is the condition of hypnosis. Here a subject is hypnotized and told, let us say, that he is at the North Pole. Immediately thereupon, to all appearances, he finds himself there with every circumstance that he would normally consider to be appropriate to the Polar regions; in addition to which he will immediately experience any condition that the operator may think fit to suggest to him. A spectator would say that both operator and subject were in London, but the subject is convinced that he is at the Pole; because it has been suggested to him.

Again, we have the condition that we call insanity; the condition of the subject under the influence of certain drugs, of which alcohol is the most familiar, and so on. Now your normal life, as we call it, is just a state of consciousness like one of these, differing in certain respects from each of the others, as they differ one from another, but a state of consciousness. It actually consists of whatever concept you happen to form about God's world, the world of reality. The people whom you meet are the concepts, good or bad, that you form of certain perfect spiritual beings; and the objects and events that come into your life are your concepts of the world of reality; or, more accurately, your entire field of consciousness at any given moment is but the more or less false concept that you form of the world of reality; for of course anything less than complete understanding and realization of heaven is a falsity.

This brings us to the fundamental and final position that *at any given moment nothing exists as far as you are concerned but the world of reality, heaven, and the particular false concept of it that you are holding at the moment.* To understand this fundamental fact is to be on the Spiritual Basis.

Heaven is always perfect happiness and harmony, unchanging good, but your concept of it is always changing; the nearer your concept at any time is to Truth the better health and more prosperity you will have.

FREE WILL

Man has free will. You are not a marionette. You have the choice of thinking rightly or wrongly. If you choose to think rightly you will experience peace, happiness, and prosperity, but if you will think wrongly all sorts of difficulties will come into your life. To think that the will is not free takes all the savoir out of life.

Free will does not mean the ability to hold wrong thoughts and then demonstrate any kind of harmonious action that we may desire. When any wrong thought is held it is bound to demonstrate trouble unless overtaken and destroyed by treatment. Free will consists in our power to choose freely whether we will have the right thought or the other, to begin with. Obviously if a man says "I have free will and therefore I will drink this bottle of whisky and I will not let it make me drunk," he is talking nonsense. His free will lies in drinking it or refraining from drinking it. Once he has swallowed it the matter is beyond his control. And so our free will lies in choosing the right or the wrong thought, Truth or error, Love or condemnation.

The spiritual man is unlimited. He has an infinite number of sides to his nature, and here we see some of these in certain ways. A man will have his business side, his home side, another side known at his sports club, another perhaps at his church, and often these are almost like different men. The banker may be quite a different person from the father, and the golfer a different person again. Another range of aspects is seen in what we know as the variations in age. The child of five, the boy of fifteen, the man at thirty or at sixty all display different characteristics, yet they all belong to the same individual. In this case the time belief makes us think that we can only have one phase at a time, and that it cannot be repeated, but in the world of reality the spiritual man can see his fellowman at any age, at any time. In heaven, of course, he only has the good qualities belonging to any particular age, the spontaneity and charm of youth, the wisdom and mellowness of age, etc.

SPACE

What we call *space* is another limitation. It really means cut-off ness. Yet it is less complete than the time limitation. We can go backwards and forwards in space again and again. If I do not like London I can go to Birmingham, and I can then change my mind and come back again to London, but I cannot, in like manner, roam up and down the centuries. Moreover, I can think of Australia as readily as I can think of the opposite side of the room I am in. When you think of any place or any person you are present mentally with that person or in that place. The belief in physical separation is rapidly being overcome, and this overcoming we see in the form of greatly improved communications, airplanes, telephones, wireless, etc.

TIME

The fact that *time* is really an illusion means that it is just as easy to treat for a so-called past or future event as for a present condition. That is to say that you can treat now about some past trouble and completely wipe it out of existence. Suppose that some unpleasant thing happened, say in the year 1909. Very well, treat now, and first all possible consequences of that thing will be wiped out of the world today; and presently, if it is worth while, even the memory of the thing will disappear from your mind and that of everybody else. How is this possible? We have seen that this life is a state of consciousness, composed of your mental convictions. What we call the past at any moment is a present concept, or we should not be aware of it, and a present concept can be altered. As there is only one race mind the getting it out of one consciousness by treatment clears it for everyone. Do not waste time, however, in speculating on the hows and whys of these things as such exercises are purely intellectual, but try it practically and be convinced.

In the same way you can treat for any future event. If you are afraid of next year for any reason, you can treat now and alter it. If you have to make a voyage, or sit for an examination at some future period and feel nervous, treat now and secure harmony. But you must treat in the present tense, for the thing is present in consciousness. Never attempt to throw your treatment either forward or backward. "Now" is the day of salvation.

There is no trouble in getting people to see that they can treat for the future, as they have always been accustomed to do it, but at first it surprised them to know that they can treat back. Yet it is true that no matter what mistakes you may have made, they can all be put right by treatment.

If it is a voyage next winter, realize, "I am surrounded by peace. All is harmony and love." If it is an examination, "I am divine spirit. I have peace and freedom. I express omniscience and Infinite Intelligence. I work quickly and well."

If it is an old sad thing of many years ago realize, "All in Spirit. This is not true. I know only harmony, peace, and spiritual success. Only divine harmonious activity is going on. All my conditions are spiritual."

It does not matter what has happened in the past, you can wipe it out.

The only exception to this law is that the dead who have passed on some time cannot be brought back. (See later lesson.)

This disposes of the melancholy complaint so often heard, "Oh, if only I had known of this teaching sooner." Never say that again. You can put everything right now.

WHY DO WE TREAT?

Why do we treat at all? Our duty to God is to maintain a calm, loving, serene state of mind. While we are in this state no harm can come to us. Trouble of any kind will always be preceded by the loss of this serenity, once we have begun to obtain some degree of dominion, and so we know that we are not safe as long as we are perturbed. This is why you must treat for little things as well as big—for a dropped teacup as well as for an earthquake.

If you see someone doing wrong, treat to clear the error out of your own mind, and get rid of the thought of censure. You must never hold a thought of condemnation.

DENIALS

Now that you are on the Spiritual Basis you can use the *denial* with understanding and terrific force. When you have severe pain you can say, "There is no pain," and really mean it, and it will sooner or later disappear. There is only heaven and your false concept of it, including, at the moment, pain; and you know that heaven is the reality.

Denials have a cleansing effect. Often it will be helpful to deny all sorts of things, even if they seem to have no direct bearing on the matter in hand.

If you are intuitive (and if not you must cultivate it by treatment, "God is inspiring me. I know everything necessary. I understand.") you will often sense what the patient's real trouble is.

AFFIRMATIONS

The *affirmation* is the power of the Logos that you, as a child of God, possess. Everything you decree you get. All the trouble in your life you have yourself ordered at some time by misusing this power, so watch your words, and do not affirm anything that you do not want to have come to pass. When you invert the power of the Logos by speaking the word for evil, you wrest it to your own destruction. The power of the "word" goes, whether you "mean" it or not. Be careful of your tongue.

If you say, "I am a bad sleeper," you are decreeing a thing, and it will be done unto you. You will sleep badly.

ARGUMENTATIVE FORM OF TREATMENT

This may be called the stock form of treatment. It is the most powerful, though not always the quickest form. It is absolutely certain to succeed, however sooner or later, and it is only a question of keeping it up long enough in order to overcome any difficulty, no matter what. The only possibility of failure lies in your getting tired or discouraged before enough work has been done. If you will only keep it up the trouble, no matter what it is, must yield; provided only that your are not attempting to bring someone back from the next plane. Any trouble on this plane must go.

It may be called the argumentative form, and it consists essentially in carrying on an argument with your own mentality until you have convinced yourself (chiefly, of course, your subconscious self) of the Truth about the matter in question; namely, harmony; for as you now know your conviction is always demonstrated. Now this form of treatment is of no use to anyone who is not on the Spiritual Basis, because they have no basis to argue from. Unless you are on the Spiritual Basis, such an argument would be meaningless and could therefore carry no conviction. The subconscious is extremely susceptible to argument, but in order that the subconscious shall accept it, it is essential that the conscious mind shall give its assent, otherwise the thing falls flat. It is not necessary that you should have any conscious optimism about the matter, to begin with, only your reason must formally assent, at least, and it could not do that until you were on the Spiritual Basis.

It will be useful to note here, the ascending value of the three principal forms of treatment given. The first can be used by anyone who believes in God and in prayer. The second demands a little more than this, as it calls for at least a slight feeling of devotion, while this, the third, necessitates the Spiritual Basis.

In practice use any form of treatment that you feel led to, and use them all if necessary. Do not in any way stand on ceremony in the matter. The course of an argumentative treatment is like this.

Let us suppose it is a case of rheumatism. Say: "Treatment can overcome this trouble. I have nothing to deal with but my own thoughts."

"I am Divine Spirit so I cannot have pain. My body is Divine Spirit so it must be perfect. God never made this trouble so it has no reality. I am not afraid of it, for I know I have dominion. I have perfect peace." Take up any symptoms that may occur to you.

Supposing you are organizing a concert or some such function. Realize, "This concert is really a divine activity; therefore it must be successful. All the people who ought to be there are spiritual beings and spiritual beings are always in their right place, so they will be there. The idea would not have emerged had there not been a need for it, and there is no power to keep away the people who would benefit by coming. So it must succeed and I am convinced that it will. Love is God and Love is always active for Love is Life and so Love must be actively demonstrated here."

Hold these thoughts until you begin to feel

some degree of conviction, and success is certain. You must on no account think of any particular person coming. There may be people whom you would like to see there, or people whom you think ought to be there, but that is really none of your business. When you treat you must leave things to God.

If you have a school, or a shop, or a nursing home, or an agency, or any professional clientele, the treatment is practically the same as this, because the need is the same; namely the coming together of unknown people for a specific purpose. You want pupils or customers or clients whom you can help.

TREATING FOR OTHERS

As an almost universal rule it is inadvisable to offer to treat for another person. Let them ask you. If you are working rightly you will have all the work coming to you that you need. As with all human rules there will be occasional good exceptions to this one. If in doubt, treat for wisdom.

Of course you will treat everything a patient tells you with the most sacred confidence. If he wishes to tell you all about his troubles let him do so, once. Do not check him however long the story may be, but reverse all the error as he goes along in this way. If he says, "That man hated me," think, "No, there is nothing but love." If he says, "I have not a penny in the world," think, "You have abundance." If he says, "I always have headaches," think, "No, you are divine spirit, and you know it." And so on. Let him have his say out and get it off his chest. Then give him an oral treatment by explaining to him that his true nature is divine and perfect and that there is nothing to be afraid of, and you will usually finish by giving a silent treatment. The next time he comes if he has anything new to say about his troubles, hear it fully and reverse it as before, but do not let him go over the old ground again. Tell him about Lot's wife.

Never be tempted to give your patients material advice. That is not your business. On the material level they must be presumed to know more about their affairs than you do.

"Should I leave home?"

"Should I sell this business?" Treat them for wisdom, and show them how to treat themselves for guidance.

Should symptoms be handled separately? Yes. Know the truth about every error that presents itself, but do not go looking for error.

Do not treat separately for the various parts of the body, unless there is something wrong with them.

WHY ARE PRAYERS NOT ANSWERED

Prayer is thinking about God, but often people think they have been praying when really they have been thinking over their troubles and telling them to God. When you work in the right way, and yet do not make your demonstration, it simply means, not that the treatment has failed, but simply that you have not yet done enough work. Go on, and sooner or later you must get your result.

Give an absent treatment exactly as though the patient were in the room with you. Do not try to "send" the treatment to him.

Treat a "chronic ailment" exactly as any other but work against the time belief, discouragement, and habit. "We are in eternity now and all is joy. God is continually creating afresh every instant so there is no stale habit."

Why are many sincere Christians invalids? They have sincerity but not understanding. They think the disease real, and that God sends it for a good purpose. We get what we believe in.

Happily the race mind is not on the side of disease in any particular case. It thinks *limitation* for everybody, but it never thinks disease for any individual. On the contrary it thinks a standard human body perfect in form and functioning, and all disease is an individual effort of wrong thinking against the current. So all that we have to do really is to let go (subconsciously) the error. The Race Mind thinks John Smith cannot live without food or stay under water indefinitely under any circumstances, but it never thinks that John Smith must necessarily have, say, tuberculosis, only that given certain circumstances he must have it. This is why it is so much easier to overcome disease than limitation.

You will not demonstrate very much unless you are honestly trying to live up to the best that you know. You may not be succeeding very well, but if you are really doing your best that is enough. A sense of unworthiness does more than anything else to keep us from demonstrating, but if you are doing your best to be what you would like to be there is no need to feel unworthy.

A treatment consists in realizing that the patient is spiritual and perfect now.

Do not expect to begin your treatment with a realization. Be thankful if you get it when you have done the work.

In treating yourself the important thing is to work for yourself exactly as though you were someone else. The danger in self-treatment is that one is apt to scamp the work. The thought is, "I know these things. I accept the truth." This however is not enough. It is not sufficient to accept the truth; you must eat it and drink it. Several good workers have passed-on prematurely because they had so many patients that they did not work enough for themselves. In working for yourself you must learn to rise above all moods, fancies and temperamental conditions. No matter what you may feel at the moment, you can always make statements of Truth, and these will do their work. Regard yourself as a patient who has come to you for treatment. A grave peril with many people is that under pretence of treating themselves they simply think intensively of their malady. Of course this only makes things much worse because "what you think on, grows."

ANOTHER FORM OF TREATMENT

When you want something, affirm steadily and quietly that your real self has it now. Or, rather that it has the spiritual reality of the thing wanted. This is simple affirmation done without regard to the feeling nature and it is often effective. "I have so and so now."

RACE MIND

We have seen that there is one common race mind, and that it works through each of us as the mind of the pianist works through his fingers. The general history of mankind is the outpicturing of the race beliefs. When man first appears he has, so to speak, tuned right out from the realization of God, and as he gradually comes back in understanding, or tunes-in again, we see everything improving. This is what constitutes "Evolution," or the progress of the

The Science of Living

human race. The teaching of natural science on the subject of evolution is an accurate description of what is seen as taking place on the surface of things, but the natural scientist is mistaken in thinking that the so-called forces of nature are causative. Nothing is causative but thought; "nature" is only our race-thoughts externalized. Things seem to improve, but it is we who are getting nearer to God in our thinking, and are therefore seeing things more truly.

The race, as a whole, is now thinking better thoughts than it formerly did, and so we see civilization instead of barbarism. This improvement will continue at a greater and greater rate until the full realization of God comes. This will be the end of all sin, disease, and limitation, i.e., the end of matter. This consummation will probably come rather suddenly, for it is the balance of thought that counts; when enough people know the Truth to counterbalance the mass of error thought, the end will come. This destruction of matter will be seen in the form of earthquakes, tidal waves, typhoons, tornadoes, etc. Nevertheless those who are on the Spiritual Basis will probably be able to wipe out the worst of it by treatment, and so things will not be nearly so bad as would otherwise be the case. Jesus foresaw what would happen and described it in Mark 13 and Luke 21. Those of us who are on the Spiritual Basis are called the Elect in the Bible.

Every time you give a treatment you help the patient, you help yourself, and you help the whole world by improving the Race Mind.

Remember that the whole thing is a network of thoughts; that, and nothing more. If it were possible for the whole human race to be annihilated, then the material world would cease to exist, simply because there would be no one to think it, for that is all there is of it. Suppose that you dreamed last night that you were present at a football match in which you were greatly interested. Suddenly your alarm clock went off and you found yourself at home in bed. What became of the football match? It was annihilated when that state of consciousness came to an end. It may be asked who was there to think the world in the days before animal life appeared on it? The answer is that the very idea that there ever were such times is part of man's present belief.

Past events can be seen and future events can

be foreseen. There are two ways of doing this; a right and a wrong way. The wrong way is what usually goes under the name of clairvoyance. This is most unreliable for several reasons and is simply an extension of material vision into the etheric realm. Sometimes it is what it purports to be; more often it is simply a reading of the subconscious of the sitter. Often it is a partial reading of some quite other person with whom the patient has recently come in contact. Sometimes it is a fantasy built up (quite unwittingly) by the clairvoyant herself.

The true mode of working is that used by Jesus. He worked spiritually by realizing that man expresses omniscience, and as he walked down the streets of Jerusalem he could read everybody's mind, past, present, and future, whenever he wanted to. If any trouble is foreseen it can be wiped out by treatment, no matter what it is. If you were correctly seen by a clairvoyant as being in, say, a railway accident next month or next year, you could treat and wipe it out so that there would be no such accident. If you were treating for yourself every day in the right way, you would receive an intuitive warning of such a thing as that in time to wipe it out.

Such a warning would probably take the form of fear. You would get clouds of fear coming over you or acute depression, or it might take the form of anger. Then you would find yourself getting very cross over something that was really trifling. When such a thing happens the proper thing to do is to treat, and if necessary get help as well, until your usual state of equanimity is restored; then you are safe. The thing foreseen is what will happen unless treatment is done. If anyone had foreseen the Great War centuries ago they would have seen the events as being even worse than they really were; because all the prayers said all over the world since then would have operated to improve the event. If enough prayer had been said the war could have been prevented altogether. Unfortunately few of the prayers said are Scientific Prayers (i.e. treatment) and the other kind is not very efficient.

As you advance in understanding you will find that certain things will happen. Poverty will gradually disappear from your life, if it has been there. You will find that you are eating less. If you smoke, that will fall away. There is nothing sinful in smoking, but it is neither a clean nor a healthy habit, and it goes. You will find that you eat much less meat, and sooner or later you will probably find that you will drop it altogether. Most important, you will find that things will cease to annoy you. When people do wrong you will not approve the wrong but you will cease to judge the wrongdoer. Instead of feeling indignant you will look upon them as we do upon naughty children—that is, without ill feeling. At last if you gain sufficient understanding you will reach what the Bible call the Millennium. This is the stage when you will have no worries or troubles of any kind; health, peace, abundance, and harmony will be yours, and you will, on account of the advanced stage of your understanding, be able to help tremendously everyone who calls upon you. The Millennium stage will come to the more advanced individuals first, but ultimately to the whole Human Race.

Certain people have been sufficiently advanced to dematerialize and go straight to heaven without dying. They first dematerialized the physical body, and then the psyche. Enoch did this, and also Moses, Elijah and John. Jesus could have done the same, but he preferred to pass through death in order to help the whole human race. That is why he is justly entitled the Savior of the World.

DEATH

What we call *death* is this; the psyche is attached to the physical body by an etheric ligament called in the Bible the "silver cord." Under certain circumstances the psyche can pass out of the body (which it really interpenetrates) and travel for long distances, returning again at any time. This is what happens during sleep (though it often remains quite near the body) and also in various forms of trance. Death is the severing of the silver cord. When that happens, the psyche, now completely detached, remains on this plane for a period of time that varies from two or three to fourteen or fifteen days, when it passes on to the next plane. If, before it passes on, someone sufficiently advanced treats about it, the silver cord can be rejoined and the subject restored, and this is called "raising the dead." Once the psyche passes over to the next plane it cannot be brought back.

The next plane is etheric. That is to say, it is

a network of thoughts as this one is, but there being no heavy physical matter everything is more vivid, more immediate, and more direct. We go to the sort of place and among the sort of people for whom we have prepared ourselves by our habitual thinking here. The day after "death" the psyche is precisely the same as it was the day before, except for the all-important knowledge that there is no death. You can pray for those who have passed on and they can pray for you. Treat for them exactly as though they were on this plane but out of sight, say in Australia. If you get a very clear realization of the oneness of Mind you can get an interior intuitive sense of communication with the one who has passed on, and even, receive a definite message. This is not psychic, but spiritual,. Your real self is always in heaven as is the real self of the other.

If when you are treating, you get a very clear realization of Spiritual Being, you may once or twice momentarily transcend the limits of time and space and matter altogether, and then you will know, not as mere knowledge, but as experience, that God really is all in all; and that you and your fellow men really are one. This is called the Cosmic Consciousness and it is a foretaste of heaven. There is a counterfeit however, an emotional state of ecstasy which is highly dangerous. You need never confuse the two, for all genuine spiritual experience is clear, calm and peaceful, without excitement or sense of hurry.

CLIMATE

The world we know is the objectified embodiment of our thoughts. Climate weather, and the seasons are the expression of the whole race thought and not merely local thinking. Arabia is a very hot country and Lapland a very cold one, because the whole race mind thinks cold weather in Lapland and hot weather in Arabia, not merely the natives of these countries. As the race thought improves the world climate will change for the better. As man gains more and more dominion over his own thoughts he will become independent of fixed seasons and times and climates.

ANIMALS

The animals as we know them are but our concepts of God's ideas. Some beasts are savage because we think them so, but it is Adam who names them —puts that seeming nature upon them (Genesis 2:19). All the death and cruelty of the jungle is in man's thought. As we spiritualize our thinking all this will change, until the lamb literally lies down with the lion, as foretold.

Animals are very easy to treat for; except in the case where it is desired to keep an aged animal alive beyond the usual span. This is difficult and unwise. It is a really a sin to fix the affections inordinately upon anything but God.

FLOWERS

Flowers are very easy to treat for. Test this in practice by purposely treating for certain plants and not for others under similar conditions.

CONCENTRATION

You must train yourself in concentration if you wish to do good work. Many people begin to treat, and then find after the lapse of some time, that the mind has wandered away from the subject in hand and that they have not actually been treating for a number of minutes.

Sometimes they have only a limited time to devote to treatment, and yet three-quarters of that time is wasted in this way. In addition to wasting time, this mind wandering has a debilitating effect upon the mentality. On the other hand interruptions during treatment, if they come from the outside, do no harm. If you are treating and the telephone rings, do not get annoyed; answer it, say or do what is necessary, and then continue your treatment. Often you will find that such an interruption is the signal that you have done enough. If so, you will feel this.

Mind wandering is not difficult to overcome provided that you do not make a bogey of it. The thing to do is this. At the beginning of the treatment hold the thought for a moment. "I am always thinking rightly; the Christ is guiding me." Then go on treating. When you notice that your attention has wandered, immediately switch it back to the treatment and continue as before the interruption. Do not pause a moment to reproach yourself for the lapse, or to make good resolutions, or to calculate how much time you have lost; go straight on. A week or two of this practice will make a great difference.

The Science of Living

Remember that mental concentration has nothing to do with pressure or vehemence. In the physical world concentration always means pressure, as in the drill or the knife, but in the mental world concentration means fidelity to a given subject. Forget the drill and think instead of a camera. If you are giving a time exposure in a dim room it is necessary to hold the object to be photographed steadily in front of the lens for a given time. If you get tired however and hold different things in front of the lens, a blurred smudge will be the result. Now our conscious minds are very much like the lens of a camera the plate of which is the subconscious. What you hold before the lens will come out on the plate. If you want a clear image on your plate hold the object steadily in front of the lens. Do not hold up anything that you do not want reproduced on the plate; sin, disease, and death, for instance. The subconscious (the plate) will objectify itself as your daily life.

You will see that the camera analogy does away with any question of pushing or gripping. You do not get a photograph by pushing the object strenuously against the lens; you are taking a photograph, not drilling through a wall.

You should treat yourself every day for these seven things: understanding, wisdom, purity, supply, love, right place, and freedom from influence. You work for these things by realizing that your real self, Pneuma, already possesses them in the fullest measure.

UNDERSTANDING. Think, "I have perfect understanding. I understand what God is, and what I am, and what my fellow man is, and what the world is. I understand everything I need to know perfectly," and so on.

For WISDOM. "I express perfect wisdom, I am guided by God. I cannot make any mistakes for I am ever about His work. There is only one plan, His plan. God designs and He executes everything. I am always acting rightly."

For PURITY realize, "I am divine spirit, all my conditions are spiritual, my body is spiritual, and only God's thoughts can come to me. In Him I live, and move, and have my being. I understand what purity is quite clearly. I have perfect serene peace." Purity is so important because its opposite, sensuality, is the strongest form of the belief in matter. Most people need to treat a good deal for understanding of what purity is, and this is often the quickest way to demonstrate it. Purity is not a merely negative thing.

Treat yourself for SUPPLY until all fear of poverty has gone.

Treat every day and many times a day for LOVE. The importance of this cannot be over-estimated. Love conquers every difficulty. If only you could love enough you would be the happiest and the most powerful person on earth.

Work for RIGHT PLACE every day, whether you are at present satisfied or not. "I am always in my right place. I express perfect harmony and perfect activity. I am always with the right people. My surroundings are perfect in every way. I am surrounded with beauty and happiness. I radiate love and service. I am thrilling with joy. I am just where I am needed."

People are often influenced by others to their detriment. You get a good idea and someone throws cold water upon it, or you are brought into contact with something or someone who would really be helpful to you, but you are preju-diced against it by a third person or by family traditions, or by educational bias, and so on. Many advertisements constitute suggestions of disease.

149

All around us are suggestions of limitation of every kind. Protect yourself from things of this sort by realizing every day, "I am divine spirit. There is positively no influence but God." Some people are very fearful of other people's thoughts influencing them secretly. The above treatment faithfully used will prevent anything of this kind. Remember that the simplest and strongest protection from evil of any kind is just a heart full of love for your fellow man.

In all the above treatments, of course, as in all treatments, "I" means Pneuma, your real self, not the limited human counterfeit.

MEDITATION

Meditate often on the Seven Main Aspects of God. This makes a very good treatment. "God is Life, and I express that Life, and understand it, etc."

Often treat for power to treat. "I am thinking rightly now. I express perfect spiritual activity." This is like sharpening your knife.

When you have some difficult or tiresome work to do, instead of gritting your teeth and going at it by will power, leave it for a little and say quietly, "I express perfect spiritual activity."

You will find it will come quite easily then.

In treatment be crisp. Do not try to just to fill up time.

Never force treatment. Stop if it becomes a burden.

Do not wrestle with the error. Know that it is not there.

Be careful to avoid mind wandering at the beginning of a treatment if you can. The first few seconds are golden.

If you cannot settle down easily to treatment, try treating for a whole string of things. "There is no worry, fear, anger, time, space, etc. All is peace, harmony, order, right activity," and so on.

The only thought that matters is the present one. We have not to worry about the thoughts of yesterday or tomorrow. If the present thought is clear enough it will heal anything.

The Second Advent is the coming of this, the Christ Truth, all over the world.

FIVE POINTS OF TREATMENT

There are five points that should be taken up in every case that you treat for, namely: FEAR,

SEX, SENSE OF SIN, INFLUENCE OF
OTHERS, and TIME.

FEAR is the arch-enemy. Take this up first in every case. As you overcome the sense of fear the case will rapidly improve. The treatment against fear is love. Perfect love casts out fear altogether. He that feareth is not made perfect in love. Treat yourself against fear many times a day. Get rid of fear and you are safe.

SEX. This is quite different thing from treating for purity and is often overlooked. It is necessary for this reason. We are all brought up in a civilized community that is (necessarily and rightly to a large extent) full of taboos and evasions in connection with this subject, but this fact necessarily leads to repression, much false shame and all sorts of subconscious terrors and doubts about sex. Needless to say this is in no way a reflection on the patient. It is chiefly subconscious thinking that we have to deal with, and one is as completely unaware of what is going on in one's subconscious as, let us say, a savage is of the complicated process of digestion proceeding in his interior. Rather the more delicate minded and conscientious a person is concerning this subject, the greater is the likelihood of repression, unconscious fear, and consequent injury.

Medical science has now discovered that all sorts of unexpected troubles are really traceable to disturbances of the sexual nature. It is believed that the sex glands, aside from their primary function, probably have a considerable influence on the general metabolism of the body in all adults, and hence any disarrangement in rhythm may have a deleterious effect. Realize, "There is no sex trouble of any kind, because man is spiritual. There is no fear in connection with sex; all is peace and happiness."

THE SENSE OF SIN. The sense of our own unworthiness is one of the two or three principal things that keep us back from God. The patient may have every reason, humanly speaking, for a bad conscience, or the reverse may be the case. Usually the better the man the more unworthy he thinks himself. Often the sense of sin is altogether subconscious. In any case treatment will clear it up. "Man knows the truth, and has peace and harmony."

TIME. The time illusion is the cause of all sadness, low spirits, and feeling of discouragement. It pretends that some good thing is now lost beyond recovery. Also handle the "getting older" thought. Man is in eternity now. In heaven anyone always has any good thing that he can think of. No loss of any kind.

CHILDREN

Children are very susceptible to treatment. A few minutes a day spent in treating for a child will make all the difference. In the general treatment for a child include general health, dealing specifically with anything that may be wrong, and take up the various points already mentioned, including supply.

Avoid discussing a child in its presence. Be very careful to avoid all negative conversation in the child's presence. As a rule do not discuss money matters in front of the child. If you are in financial difficulties especially, be careful not to discuss them in front of him, or to let him know more about them than is necessary. The child cannot help you to solve the problem, and by bringing him into it you are helping to impress him with a poverty consciousness.

In case of a sick child treat the people around the child, especially the mother, or whoever is taking the place of the mother. If the child is under a year old give at least fifty percent of the treatment to the mother.

To help children with their school work, realize Intelligence, Wisdom, and Love for the child.

To protect young people from bad company either at school or later on, is not difficult. It is a wonderful thing to know that you can sit quietly at home and protect the boy or girl who may be many miles away in some distant city. Realize that he (she) is divine spirit, and only God's thoughts can come to the real man. Then realize Wisdom and Love as never absent.

When a child commits a fault do not heap reproaches upon it. Realize divine perfection, and explain rationally the undesirability of the wrong course. Change your thought about the child and the child will change.

In explaining Truth to a child do not attempt to "gear down" as it were, to what you think is the child's level. Tell the child the whole truth about God. Children get the spiritual idea quite easily. Children treat very successfully and should be taught to clear up most of their own little difficulties themselves.

You can treat for a public cause just as well as for an individual. Sometimes it is even easier. You can treat for, say, a missionary society, a club, a commercial company, or the nation. Work for harmony and wisdom, and whatever you think is needed. If you treat for any controversial thing such as an election, you must not take sides while you are treating. Realize harmony and be willing that the best for the country must happen. Your private views may be wrong.

As a lifetime of the human being unfolds we find that two major crises are experienced. The one on passing from childhood to maturity, and the other about the season called middle age. These are, as we know they must be, both physiological and psychological in their nature. They are often periods of great storm and stress, but needless to say, this is not necessary. Realize that the Spiritual Individual knows no crisis. He is and feels unchanging spiritual harmony from everlasting to everlasting. No change in character of functioning, always perfect. All is peace, harmony, and joy. Work against fear and suggestion because the general thought invests simple, natural things with many imaginary terrors.

There must of course be no attempt to resist as it were these changes in the material person. For the time being scientific demonstration will consist in the harmonious development of the body along the recognized path of physiology, but the way to ensure this by treatment is to realize that the Spiritual Individual changes not.

BODY FUNCTIONS

For indigestion, constipation, and other functional irregularities work against fear, resentment and indignation, all of which may be altogether subconscious and unsuspected by the patient. These things have a paralyzing effect on the system. Realize Love and Harmony, and know that God is the only cause and that the action of God must be unfailingly and immediately successful. No stagnation in mind. All is perfect rhythmical activity.

THE BIBLE

The Bible is written in symbol and allegory because that form is the only one that would enable it to appeal to people of every race and every age, and every degree of intellectual and spiritual advancement.

As you advance in understanding you can go back to one of these inspired allegories and get more and more out of it time and again.

There are a few general keys running throughout the Bible, and when once you are possessed of these keys you can work out most of the other things for yourself.

The Bible is the story of man's tuning of himself back into the true consciousness of God. This story is told again and again in all sorts of different ways, and from many different angles, but it is always the same story.

The central theme in the Old Testament is the history of Israel—Israel the man and Israel the nation. Israel is really Everyman. That is to say, Israel is anyone anywhere who believes in God and in the efficacy of prayer. Those who know how to pray scientifically are called in the Bible the Elect, but if you pray in any way you are Israel. Israel starts as Jacob, and Jacob is not at all a likeable person; he is essentially selfish. But a change comes over Jacob one day; he meets the wrestling angel in the darkness, and refusing to give up the fight he struggles all night and at last prevails. After that he is no longer the same man. His nature is changed, and he gets a new name too. His new name Israel means *a prince with God*. He now realizes his divine sonship. *Israel* is compounded of three words Is, Ra, and El. Is represents the feminine principle or inspiration, you hear it when you take a deep breath, Ra (the Egyptian God) stands for the masculine, executive principle, and El represents the complete name for God. The history of Israel the nation is the going down into Egypt, the land of bondage, the escape from there across the Red Sea, the wandering in the wilderness, and the possession (incomplete) of the Promised Land. Here again is described the history of the human race as a whole, and the history of every one of us individually.

The name of a person or thing is an indication of its nature. All the place names, as well as personal names, in the Bible have a meaning. When a person's nature is radically altered his or her name is altered too. Hence Jacob becoming Israel; Abram, Abraham; Sara, Sarah; Saul, Paul, etc. Hence too, the custom of giving children their names at Baptism.

Egypt means belief in matter; in its various

forms as limitation, belief in weather and climate, drugs and medicine. Diets and so on. Babylon means matter in the more subtle etheric form as seen in hypnotism, etc.

Water stands for the human mind (psyche) and to cross water is to get a victory over the human mind by rising to a higher level of consciousness.

Colors, too, have a meaning, the three primary colors standing for the three main aspects of God. Orange-yellow for Life; red for Love, and blue for Truth. The Red Sea is the most difficult crossing the soul makes, and red stands here for human passion as being the counterfeit or perverted seeing of the true Love. Truth gives us peace, and the blue sea is always the calm one.

The beginning of trouble is referred to in the Bible as a mist (water in its most subtle form) going up and watering the whole earth. In Psalm 23 we read, "He leadeth me by the still waters" (the soul at peace). Again we read, "When the waves arise thou stillest them."

Jesus, who demonstrated completely over the human mind, was able actually to walk on the waters, literally putting them under his feet.

And so on through the Bible; look it up for yourself.

When you reach the millennium stage what do you find? Round the throne of God the Sea of Glass, or perfect smoothness, and that is the prelude to the time when there shall be no more sea.

The *mountain* means prayer or uplifted thought. The top of the mountain is the realization of God alone. All the great men in the Bible get their knowledge of Truth on a mountain.

The valley or the plain means unhappiness or sin. "I will lift up mine eyes unto the hills from whence cometh my help." When Lot was fleeing from destruction he was told, "Fly to the mountain and do not look back."

In the Bible where you get a man and wife together they really stand for the human being. Everyman. The man represents the body and the woman the mind or psyche. The man the intellect and the woman intuition.

The story of the Garden of Eden is the greatest of all the allegories. It was never meant to be taken literally. Adam and Eve are Everyman. Note that it was Eve who brought trouble upon

Adam. We know why from our metaphysical studies. It is the psyche that brings trouble on the body. No error can appear on the body until it is first in the soul. The body is only the externalization of the thoughts in the soul. Adam cannot bring trouble on Eve. Only Eve can eat the forbidden fruit.

Now that you are on the Spiritual Basis you understand that you have nothing to deal with but your own thoughts; and that whatever beliefs you accept will be expressed in your body and surroundings. The only way to be free is to decline to accept error on any terms, and this means refusing to taste the fruit of the tree of the knowledge of good and evil. No one is likely to waste time on anything that they suppose to be wholly evil; it is the delusion of good in evil that tempts people.

The Tree of Life is the knowledge of the allness of good; and that is the tree whose leaves are for the healing of the nations.

The important women of the Bible all stand for various states of the soul. *Eve* is the fallen soul; *Mary Magdalene* the redeemed soul; *the Virgin Mary* the perfect (virgin) soul. The Christ consciousness is born in the virgin (pure) soul.

The Science of Living

Israel (ourselves) is told to go in and possess the Land, but, instead, he spends years in the wilderness. We do this because instead of treating faithfully about everything we rely too often upon our own efforts and opinions.

Israel was told that he could claim any land that he put his foot upon. *The Land* is manifestation. The *foot* is concentration, which you will see is also understanding. Whatever you understand spiritually you will come to possess in manifestation. Any lack anywhere means a lack of understanding at that point. Get your understanding and you will get what you want.

Wine stands for Spirit.

The wrath of God means the activity of God destroying error.

Judgment is the destruction of error, usually the activity of man destroying error by knowing the Truth.

The fear of the Lord means reverence for God.

Righteous means right thinking.

Wicked means bewitched.

The word *city* means consciousness.

Enemies and *heathens* always mean our own wrong thoughts, the only enemies we have.

The *pearl* means wisdom. Wisdom means the

knowledge of the allness of good; being on the Spiritual Basis.

A thing is in the Bible because it is true; it is not true because it is in the Bible.

We are all engaged in building a spiritual consciousness, and in the Bible the great building is Solomon's Temple. This structure, founded on a rock, is a wonderful allegory of the human consciousness. The remarkable thing about it is that it had to be built in perfect silence; in other words, thought is the builder. The soul is built in silence.

There were five things found around the temple: the gold and the silver, the ivory, the apes, and the peacocks. These symbolize in a marvelous way the five temptations that come to the soul that is striving to be free. The actual form of the temptation will vary according to the position in life and circumstances of the subject.

The gold symbolizes lust for personal power. The true meaning of gold is the omnipresence of the availability of the divine power, which is impersonal.

The silver stands for greed of money.

Ivory stands for mistaken loyalty. It is an unselfish error, but a deadly one. Only one thing in existence has any right to your loyalty, and that is the Christ Truth within yourself. You cannot and must not recognize any loyalty to a church, a teacher or leader, a textbook, or anything but the living action of the Holy Spirit. To do so is to commit the sin against the Holy Ghost.

The ape stands for any bodily temptation, such as sensuality, drink, drugs, etc.

The peacock stands for vanity. It may be intellectual pride, or it may take the form of claiming infallibility as a teacher, for instance.

Begin *every one* of your treatments by making these two statements, no matter how many treatments you may give the day:

"Treatment can overcome this difficulty."

"I have nothing to deal with but my own thoughts." (Or, "I have nothing to deal with but the patient's thoughts," if working for another.) Never omit this.

Learn to treat anywhere, in crowds, in trains, walking about, lying in bed, at table, and so on. Learn to treat with your eyes open as they will have to be on committees, boards, etc.

If you allow yourself to harbor a single "down"

on anyone, or a grudge, or a grievance, you might just as well put a rattlesnake into your bosom; and if you indulge in habitual hatred, or contempt, or fear of any body of people whether it be a nation, a class, or a religious sect, you might as well swallow poison.

If you think you cannot treat for some particular reason, then treat that "reason." If it is "no time" treat for time. If it is a "headache" that stops you, treat the headache. If it is noise outside, treat the noise. If it is laziness (as it probably is), treat that.

If you are puzzled how to handle a certain difficulty treat for guidance (by claiming it, as usual).

If you are fearful, or worried, or tired, or discouraged, or hurt, or disappointed, or in pain, God is your sure remedy, so *treat*.

If only you will treat faithfully and regularly and try to live up to the best that you know, it is only a question of time before all troubles, all doubts and fears, all sad memories, all mistakes will fade away forever, and perfect peace and joy come into your life.

SIMPLEST FORM OF TREATMENT

The simplest form of treatment is the blessing. You see someone in trouble or you hear of it, and you simply bless them and leave it; and often the next thing you hear they are out of their trouble. If you feel moved to hold out your hand as you do so, as they do in the East, do so.

There is nothing superstitious in this. It is simply a quick summing-up of all that you know in truth about the subject.

Some people make a practice of blessing any new object that they may buy, a watch, a motorcar, a house, anything.

If anyone makes you feel very angry, bless them and leave them.

Bless the house, the room, and the city.

Never delve into the past to dredge up things to treat for.

If you feel very strongly about something do not, nevertheless, be tempted to say, "it is useless to treat about this because I am determined to do so and so tomorrow." Treat, and it will still be open to you to do what you wish to do when tomorrow comes. But—you may think better of it if you treat.

Remember that the one thing that matters is treatment. Time spent in treatment is never wasted. If you do not treat you cannot expect results. People say, "I do not actually treat much but I keep my thoughts right all day." This is self-deception of a deadly kind. If you were keeping your thoughts right you would find yourself giving much time to treatment.

Treat definitely for yourself every day or you will get nowhere.

The two things that do us the most harm are condemnation and resentment. They have to go.

The two Poles of Life are Love and Wisdom. Unite them in every activity.

Love is by far the most important of all things. Treat for Love daily. Give yourself a short treatment for it many times a day. It is the fulfilling of the Law. It casts out fear. It covers a multitude of sins. Love is absolutely invincible.

Minutes spent in treating for wisdom will save hours spent in overtaking your mistakes.

If you see a drunken man in the street it is no use to say that he is not drunk; that is nonsense. The thing to do is to refrain from condemnation; and realize that his real self,

Pneuma, is divine and perfect. If you realize this clearly enough he will become sober, and if still more clearly, he would never drink again.

If the thought of some old injury comes into your mind, bless the offender and let it go.

You will never demonstrate on something in a book; only on what is in your consciousness.

Trying to treat is treating.

Divine Love always meets every difficulty; but it can only meet it in the form of a change of thinking on your part.

"Mortal mind" or "error" is not something "attacking" you; it is just those wrong thoughts of your own.

Give a little general treatment each day for the whole world.

Such, then, in outline, is the truth about life, and about ourselves. The story, after all, turns out to be a simple one. Life is completely and utterly good, for there exists but One Presence and One Power, God, and God is perfect, infinite Love, without variableness or shadow of turning; the same yesterday, today, and forever. Anything else that may seem to be is but a passing cloud of misconception, to vanish as soon as recognized. *So there is nothing to be afraid of.*

Absolutely nothing but our own ignorance and doubt. Good is all in all, and now that we know this there remains but for us to put that knowledge into practice. Without that it is but a sounding brass and a tinkling cymbal. To know your divine sonship is but the first step; you must claim it. And prove your knowledge by demonstration. No teacher can more than point the way in which the student must himself walk, and explore, and arrive. "No man can save his brother's soul or pay his brother's debt." By constant treatment you must understand your way back to the realization of health, harmony and unfading joy, in the overcoming of the separation belief.

This class should be the turning point in your life, but you have free will and it is for you to determine what line your own future shall take. If you work in Truth you cannot help but triumph, if you do not work, as surely you will not. Remember it makes no difference what your problem is, how deep seated the trouble, how hopeless the outlook, how muddled the tangle, how great the mistake, the action of God in treatment can overcome it. But you must work.

The Science of Living

I shall always be interested to hear of any special demonstration that you make.

The Peace of God be upon your soul, and upon the whole world.

Yours in Fellowship,

EMMET FOX

Emmet Fox

Memories of Emmet Fox

The following stories were shared with us by Emmet Fox's close friends, Blanche and Herman Wolhorn, and by others who knew him and were touched not only by his teaching but by his practice of Truth.

A RICH CONSCIOUSNESS

Among the many people Dr. Fox counselled through the years was a young woman named Laura. She asked him how she could demonstrate a successful career—including fame and riches—as a musician. He replied: "First you must have a rich consciousness. Riches is not an accumulation of money but the understanding of the all-pervading Power that never fails. Whatever you form in your mind and have faith in will manifest." His final word of advice to her was, "Search for God, not fame and money; then you will have true riches." Five years passed, and one day tickets for orchestra seats arrived at the church office for Dr. Fox. They were a gift from Laura accompanied by this simple message of gratitude: "I took your advice, and it paid off." She was performing a solo with the Los Angeles Symphony, the beginning of a successful career as an acclaimed pianist.

PHYSICAL HEALING

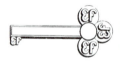 People from all walks of life asked Dr. Fox for spiritual assistance. For example, Eileen, one of the housekeepers in the building where Dr. Fox lived, stopped him one morning to ask for help. Her back was in considerable pain, making it difficult for her to perform her duties at work. She explained to Dr. Fox that she could not take time off since this job was her only means of

income. Dr. Fox asked her to sit for a few minutes. With spiritual insight, he asked her why she felt that life was such a burden. She knew right away that he was aware of her problem. She was a single mother struggling to support her young child and her mother in Ireland, while trying to save enough money to bring her family to America. Dr. Fox told her that he was going to scientifically pray for release and emotional support. His instruction to her was to practice feeling the hands of God supporting her. "Every time you feel discomfort, feel the supporting hands even more and affirm, 'God is my strength and support; Divine harmony is established in my mind and body.'" Eileen began working with this thought and gave Dr. Fox regular updates. The back pain which had once incapacitated her began to fade until it was completely gone. True to his practical nature, a year or so later, Dr. Fox arranged for Eileen's son and mother to come to live in the United States.

BUILDING FAITH

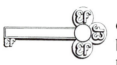

Dr. Fox once said, "Fear can paralyze both mind and body." This is a story of how he helped someone instantaneously overcome fear. Dr. Fox enjoyed taking day trips to Coney Island. He loved the fresh salt air in the early hours of the morning as he strolled along the boardwalk. Always, he stopped at Feltman's famous carousal, marveling over the vibrant sounds of the carousal organ.

On one occasion he invited his friend and colleague Florence Shinn to join him. As they strolled along the boardwalk chatting, they came upon a young mother struggling with two children. It seemed the children were anxious to ride the roller coaster. They overheard the mother, speaking in French, tell the children she was afraid to go on the ride. Dr. Fox greeted her in French and offered to take the children on the ride.

Florence Shinn later recalled that he looked straight into the young mother's face and silently extended his hand to her. Then he said in French, "There is nothing in life to fear."

With a broad smile he added, "I am an expert roller coaster rider. Come and ride." She smiled as they all stepped up to the ride. When the ride was over the smiling French woman thanked Emmet and said, "It was okay." He smiled and replied, "Yes, my dear, it is all okay."

Later, the Coney Island organ, which Emmet admired, was in much need of repair. It was sold and put on display in a museum in Baden, Germany in the Black Forest region. Dr. Fox visited that museum several times to see and hear the organ he so dearly loved.

DIVINE LIGHT AND PROTECTION

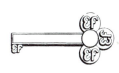 Emmet Fox knew the importance of peace of mind and knew how to help others find it. He said, "Peace of mind is positively the greatest of all God's gifts." A young woman, however, who sought emergency help from Dr. Fox did not have peace of mind. She had received a letter from the war department stating that her husband Fred was missing in action. Dr. Fox reassured her that

Infinite Wisdom knows the way out of every situation.

He listened as she spoke about her husband. He had been sent to Massena, the capitol of Sicily. He wrote to her about the endless siege and appalling conditions. He spoke of a number of casualties suffered by the men in his detail and asked her not to worry even if she did not hear from him for a while since his group was moving to a new location. Anna cried out to Dr. Fox, "He is lost, hurt and I fear he will never return home."

"Affirmations go wherever we send them," said Dr. Fox. "If you speak to your husband, he will hear you on a subconscious level." They prayed together, affirming divine order. In his prayer with Anna, he focused on Light, the illumination of Spirit residing at the center of every being. He asked her to focus on the light and continue affirming divine order. Six weeks later, Anna received word that Fred was in a hospital in Naples. He later told her that he and his men had located a dark tunnel and as they proceeded they were aware of an unexplainable shadow of light. They followed the light, which ultimately led them to safety.

"I AM HAPPY, I AM FREE"

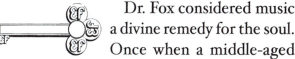Dr. Fox considered music a divine remedy for the soul. Once when a middle-aged woman sought help from Dr. Fox for depression, he wrote a little jingle for her. "I am happy, I am free, I am glad just being me." He sang this to her and asked her to sing it at least three times a day, even while she was in the shower, and promised she would experience a remarkable change in consciousness. The woman loved the little song Dr. Fox wrote for her and sang it every day. She began coming to the Sunday services with a smile on her face and eventually began looking radiant. After one of the Sunday services she whispered to Dr. Fox, "I am not sad anymore. Thank you."

RELEASE FROM THE PAST

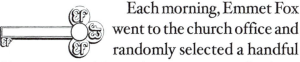Each morning, Emmet Fox went to the church office and randomly selected a handful of letters to read from the incoming mail. These he sensed were letters from people with great needs. And it seemed they always were. On one

179

occasion he opened a letter from a woman named May who lived in California. Her husband had left her, her daughter disappeared with a young man, and she was burdened with crippling arthritis. She feared being sick and alone. Dr. Fox wrote a reply, asking May to write him a letter each day, detailing as much as she could about her life. He instructed her to be specific. Then he asked her to end every letter with, "I release these thoughts. They no longer disturb me, and I now move forward." Dr. Fox said he would not open the letters but would read them spiritually. In return he would send her a prayer treatment to work with each week. He said, "Never look back. The road ahead may be bumpy, but the road back means failure. God is always in the road ahead."

May sent letters to Dr. Fox every day. She said she wrote how the joints in her hands improved from the continuous writing. She wrote for almost a year before she decided to take a trip to New York to hear Dr. Fox lecture at the Manhattan Opera House. While there, she handed one of the ushers a note for Dr. Fox. It said, "Dr. Fox, it's me your pen pal, May, from California. I am here and I am healed." After the service and before the question and answer time, Dr. Fox introduced May by asking her to join him on the platform. "This is May, my pen pal," he said. "She raised her consciousness above arthritis."

THE HEALING POWER OF LAUGHTER

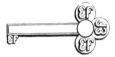 Whenever time allowed in Dr. Fox's busy schedule he would make a visit to the pediatric ward at one of the local hospitals. He would bring hand puppets and perform a puppet show for the children. He even created his own little stage from a box. It gave him great pleasure to see the children laugh at his puppet characters, each with a unique voice he created for them. Dr. Fox believed that laughter was a divine remedy, and no doubt, this proved true for many of his young friends. "If people only knew the healing power of laughter," he observed, "the doctors would soon be out of business."

STAKE YOUR CLAIM

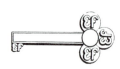 Dr. Fox often received letters from people requesting prayers for the sale of their home or prayer treatments for successful relocation. Early in his ministry, he received a letter from a man named George requesting prayer treatment for the sale of his late mother's home in Rye, New York. George explained that it had been five months and there seemed to be no sign of a buyer. The winter was approaching and he did not want to leave the house with no heat, fearing the pipes would burst. "Why are my prayers not answered?" he wrote. In his reply, Dr. Fox advised, "Release the house keys, George, and stake your claim. There must be an act of faith to achieve the desired results." George immediately removed the house keys from his key ring and again prayerfully placed the house into the hands of God. That Saturday, the real estate agent handling the property telephoned, saying, "George, we have a buyer." The house was sold.

ABSENT HEALING

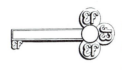 On one occasion, Edmond, a friend of Emmet Fox and the Fox family was injured in an automobile accident in a small town near London. Kirk, also a family friend and the passenger in the car went to the telegraph office to send a wire to Dr. Fox requesting immediate prayers for Edmond. When Kirk handed the clerk the telegram to be sent to Dr. Fox, the clerk said, "I have a wire that just came for you." Kirk, surprised, opened the telegram. It was from Dr. Fox assuring him of his prayers. Months later when Edmond had recovered from the accident and learned that Dr. Fox would be speaking in London, he and Kirk arranged to go to the lecture. When Edmond saw Dr. Fox he said, "Emmet, how did you know about the accident?" Dr. Fox replied, smiling, "Edmond, do you think angels have no wings?"

LOVE AND CARE FOR ANIMALS

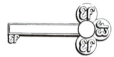 Emmet Fox enjoyed stopping at the park each morning to feed the birds and the squirrels. He was once referred to as "a host of God," because of his love and care for animals. Once, he came upon two small abandoned cats, which he named Angel and Buttercup. He began feeding the cats on a regular basis. When the cold weather set in, he sought refuge for them among the local shopkeepers. One of the store owners agreed to take both cats in and care for them. Emmet was pleased.

Some time later, a small dog appeared in front of his hotel. He began following Emmet to the park. Emmet began to feed the dog, getting some bones and meat from a local butcher shop. He asked his doorman to find out about the dog, and the doorman said it had been around for some time. Realizing it must have been lost or abandoned, Emmet tried to locate its owner without success. Early one Sunday morning when Emmet was on his way to his church service, the dog followed him. He decided to take the dog into the service. He then proceeded to set him on the platform where he would speak. The dog sat through the service without disruption. Before the end of the service Emmet Fox introduced the dog, he called Pete. He said to his congregation, "Someone here is high enough in consciousness to see above the shaggy appearance of Pete, to his beautiful soul. That someone is going to give Pete a home today." The dog was adopted that day by an affluent couple living on the West side. Later that day, Herman Wolhorn, his close friend and assistant asked Dr. Fox, "How did you come upon naming the dog Pete?"

Dr. Fox answered, "I thought, 'For Pete's sake, who would abandon such a nice animal?'"

Emmet
Fox His Life Story
JoAnn Pecoraro Corsiatto, D.Sc.F.
with Cecil Corsiatto

Long awaited—Now available!
Emmet Fox: His Life Story
by JoAnn Pecoraro Corsiatto, D.Sc.F.
with Cecil Corsiatto

For twenty years, Emmet Fox filled the ballrooms of New York hotels, Carnegie Hall, and even the Hippodrome, with thousands of people each week. They came to hear him speak on themes of success, health, and happiness and to learn about his positive interpretations of the scriptures. The author of a widely popular book, *The Sermon on the Mount*, Dr. Fox was a New Thought minister who attracted people from all walks of life. His close friends, Herman and Blanche Wolhorn, accompanied him and assisted in his work almost from the time he arrived in New York from London. The Wolhorns shared their most treasured memories of Emmet Fox with the author of this new biography, the first book about him in almost thirty years.

What made Emmet Fox so popular, and what was he really like? For the first time, this book tells the story of his private life -- his growing-up years, health, education, introduction to New Thought, friends, family, interests, likes and dislikes, and more. It tells personal stories of people he helped during his ministry and the acts of kindness he showed his friends. *Emmet Fox: His Life Story* reveals the poignant details of his transition in 1951 and his premonition of this event many years before.

This book provides fascinating insights into Emmet Fox, the man, to give you an even greater appreciation of Emmet Fox the teacher, healer, and best-selling author.

ISBN: 1-881099-35-0

We are always interested in hearing from those who have benefited from the writings of Emmet Fox. If you would like to share your experience, please write to

Revs. JoAnn & Cecil Corsiatto
Post Office Box 21
Farmingdale, New York 11735

For additional information on Emmet Fox, visit www.emmetfox.net